Me, Myself
and
Lord Byron

Me, Myself
and
Lord Byron

Julietta Jameson

PIER 9

Published in Australia in 2011 by Pier 9, an imprint of Murdoch Books Pty Limited

Murdoch Books Australia
Pier 8/9
23 Hickson Road
Millers Point NSW 2000
Phone: +61 (0) 2 8220 2000
Fax: +61 (0) 2 8220 2558
www.murdochbooks.com.au

Murdoch Books UK Limited
Erico House, 6th Floor
93–99 Upper Richmond Road
Putney, London SW15 2TG
Phone: +44 (0) 20 8785 5995
Fax: +44 (0) 20 8785 5985
www.murdochbooks.co.uk

Publisher: Colette Vella
Project Editor: Elizabeth Cowell / Elena Gomez
Editor: Anouska Jones
Designer: Emilia Toia / Tania Gomes

National Library of Australia Cataloguing-in-Publication Data

Jameson, Julietta
Me, myself and Lord Byron : a woman, a poet and a quest to
    reclaim the zest for life / Julietta Jameson
978-1-74196-645-9 (pbk.)
Jameson, Julietta, 1963—Journeys
Byron, George Gordon Byron, Baron, 1788–1824—Journeys—Europe
Journalists—Australia—Biography
Europe—Description and travel
070.92

Printed in Australia by Griffin Press, an Accredited ISO AS/NZS 14001:2004 Environmental
Management System printer.

For Gabrielle, Tony, Declan and Ronan,

who remind me of why dreams are worth pursuing.

Prologue

I am a born-again virgin. I must be. I haven't felt this nervous about a date since I was seventeen, in the hour before I went out on my very first date with my very first boyfriend, who turned into my very first lover. I am exhilarated, exactly like I was when I was getting ready to go to see *Xanadu* or whatever the film was with that boy, and this is beyond ridiculous because it's been about thirty years since then.

I qualify as a born-again virgin on another front. I am quite sure there's some statute somewhere that sets down how long a period of non-participation in carnal activity constitutes a reinstatement of virginal privileges. And under it, I could easily qualify to be sacrificed to the gods on a big open-air altar in some ancient land. Or be valued highly in certain cultures. Or marry in the Catholic church. I'm that virginal.

This is what I am thinking as I torture my hair into smoothness, quite a battle considering my hair is curly and the air is about eighty per cent humidity in Byron Bay. There's a reason why, in this high-end hippie enclave in the lush, leafy north of New South Wales, many miles from my Sydney home, the native maidens go *au naturel*, with tousled hair, no make-up and boho-chic flowing frocks. It's the damn humidity. I want to look suitably minimally made up and definitely boho-chic and flowing, and I am putting an enormous amount of effort into this devil-may-care look, double what I might usually because the sodden elements want me to look less boho, more hobo. My efforts are paying off though. I seem to be winning the battle.

I am in the pleasantly neutral bedroom of the apartment accommodation I have colonised for the weekend. My trusty MacBook is perched open on the bed and it is blaring The Killers out of my iTunes library as I move on to eye shadow and blusher. I spritz Acqua di Parma, the perfume that reminds me of *bella Italia*, the country I consider my spiritual home. The Killers too remind me of Italy these days. They have been my favourite band since I saw them at the Roman amphitheatre in Verona, only months ago. There is something about their authenticity and energy that has captured my musical heart. They remind me of my own newfound authenticity and energy as I sing along about spacemen and joy rides and the other quirky things their songs are apparently about. I don't know what it all means, except it makes me happy. And right here, right now, that's all I need.

In a mere couple of hours, I will be meeting Gabriel for the first time face to face, in the beer garden of the Beach Hotel. We have, of course, conversed a lot via email since initially encountering each other on a dating site. He lives on the coast in southern Queensland, I in Sydney, so an earlier meeting was not possible. I had reason to come to Byron Bay, by way of my work as a travel writer; it's only an hour or so from where he lives and so here, in Byron, the first meeting shall be. I've been quite taken by the way he has presented online but past experience lets me know to not bet the farm on things working out. Internet dating is an inexact science.

And that's cool, because here's the thing: it's not really the man I am so excited about. It's me. It's as if I am going on a date with my real self for the very first time. In the past six months, I have gone to the core of me, stared down my basest motivators, got my hands dirty pulling the plug on the mire of spiritual muck I've been wading in. I can't say I'm completely free, because who knows what lurks in the subconscious out of sight. But I can say I am as clear as can be right now. To the best of my current abilities, I have addressed myself. And I feel as if I know me. More than I ever have.

Of course as any snail that's lost its shell will tell you—if it lives long enough—with shell gone comes vulnerability. Vulnerability is so great, the snail will tell you, feeling all light and airy and faster than ever without that big crusty shield on its back ... until a big shoe comes along.

It's when I have moved from the bedroom of my Belongil apartment and am in the kitchen ironing my frock—bought new for my date, a floaty blue cotton floral wrap that dips and skims and falls in the right places and breathes and is so Byron Bay—that the big shoe hovers. I have not been naked with a man for some years. The last time a man saw me without clothes for the first time, I was (still only just) in my thirties. I am no longer in my thirties. I'm forty-six. Holy shit. That's a big, heavy shoe.

I have a friend I call Yentl. She is the queen of the set-up, the queen of dating advice, the queen of romance. She loves romance. Everyone needs a Yentl in their life. Some big heavy shoes can only be held up by the Yentls of this world. I put down the iron, grab my phone and call my Yentl.

3

Yentl, whose real name is Angie, is married for the second time, with an adorably bouncy, *Idol*-bound teenage daughter from her first marriage and a precious little boy from her second who has been to death's door a few times with his asthma and has made Angie all the more sensitive to happiness and the world's need for it. Her husband is one of those saintly-meets-sexy men who should be cloned.

'Darl,' she says, high pitched and thrilled. 'Thank God you called me. What time are you meeting him? Make sure you text me from the toilet with regular updates throughout the evening.'

I start crying. Annoying, because my make-up job is perfection, but also annoying because, for Heaven's sakes, it's only a date and I'm an adult and I have come so far. And I *value myself*. For the first time in my life, I do. This vulnerability caper is so, so new to me. I blurt out the nakedness thing.

'Oh, JJ,' says Angie, 'I remember when I had to start dating again. It took enormous trust and courage. I was so scared, but I had to take a big breath and get out there. You really have to,' she says.

'I know,' I say. 'Honestly, I'm ready for this. But I've never felt more guileless in my life. It's like I don't have any tricks any more. I have no choice but to be me and that is the weirdest thing for me. I've always had a big old bag of tricks. I've had tap dances, jokes, magic tricks, whoopee cushions, smoke bombs; metaphorically speaking, you know, the big jokey diversions, the show-offy stuff, the disappearing act. Now all I have is me. I don't know how to be anything *but* me any more.'

'You're ready, that's all. You're ready for the real deal.'

'I know,' I say quietly.

'This bloke might not be it,' says Angie. 'He might be, but there's a good chance he won't be. What he is, though, is the beginning of you being out there, ready for the real thing. He's also a possibility though. I mean, I would love it if he was the real deal. I only ask you don't retreat again if he's not the one. Promise me you won't.'

'I couldn't retreat now if I tried.'

It's the truth. I have now put myself so far out onto the path that there's no turning back.

My journey to this point began nearly two years earlier with a decision to address the way and amount I was drinking. Like so many single women in their forties, I'd come to rely on alcohol as the companion I didn't have, nor was at all aware I wanted. I should have been aware then. Things like reruns of *Mad About You* would make me want to top up my wine glass. That cute, smart, totally in love New York couple made me want to drink. It shouldn't have taken a person who regards herself as reasonably intelligent a few years to work out what that meant.

The journey I chose would be, without question, the most painful of my life and I had clocked up a few nasty episodes in my forty-five years prior: two car accidents, one near financial ruination, three retrenchments, several dead pets, an episode with the federal police thanks to the unbeknown-to-me criminal doings of a short-term lover, three major relocations, the divorce of my parents, several failed significant relationships, the death of an estranged father, the death of an adored mother. None of them compared to the pain of rebirth from my encroaching emotional dependence on alcohol. But of course, all of them, every single one of them, had their part to play in the crisis and they would have their role in the healing.

The healing had been what had brought me to this point, on a late spring Friday afternoon in Byron Bay, ironing a new dress for a first date with a man from the Queensland coast. The healing had also been a journey of a lifetime; not only an emotional trip, but one that physically took me travelling to northern Europe for one very special, transformational summer.

I've done a lot of travel in recent years, having been lucky enough to manoeuvre my career into a place where travel writing is now part of my bread and butter. One day I was emailing with my favourite editor, Sarah at *The Sun-Herald*'s travel section, after I had filed a story on a hotel called the Lord Byron in Rome.

'Here's an idea,' I wrote to Sarah. 'Me following in the footsteps of Lord Byron around Europe.'

'You know, that's a really great idea. You should do it,' she answered.

And that was how I suddenly had this calling to follow the adventures of a poet, perhaps the nineteenth century's most famous poet, George Gordon, Lord Byron. Though the kernel of the idea appeared so effortlessly, it *had* been a calling. In the kitchen at Belongil, as I hung up from Angie and went back to getting ready for my date, I reflected on that.

One minute, it had been this great idea. Hey, why don't I go follow in the footsteps of Lord Byron around Europe? Seemingly the next, it was like I had gone through a magic metamorphism machine and been spat out the other end, a new version of myself.

I followed Byron because I knew and loved him from my childhood. What he did while I traced his trail was introduce me to me. See, Byron was many things, but above all, he was a man who knew himself. Getting willingly close to him and his story, the self-knowledge apparently rubbed off more than a teensy bit.

Lord Byron left England in 1816—a decision born of scandal—and would never return. His self-exile seemed an appropriate landmark to me. I too wanted to exile myself from inauthenticity, cut ties with the emotional stuff that no longer served me. Firstly I went to Geneva, because after crossing from England by ship, then travelling through Belgium by coach, the first place Lord Byron settled was in a rented villa on Lake Geneva in Switzerland for five months. Then he moved on to Venice and its surrounds, on the north-eastern Italian coast, stopping briefly in Milan on the way, so I did too. As he spent several years in the Veneto a good deal of my time was spent there also.

From Venice he moved to Ravenna on the Adriatic coast as did I, and then on to Tuscany on the west coast, where Byron holed up in Pisa for a bit as well as spending a few months in Montenero and Genoa in Liguria. I put Pisa on my itinerary with the intent of exploring those other areas from my Pisan base.

When he left Italy after some six years, Byron captained a boat from Genoa to the Ionian island of Cephalonia before heading to the Greek mainland at Messolonghi. This was where he died. And so I went to those places too, ending my own sojourn where his life journey ended.

As I had three months to spare for the trip, I divided it up in accordance with the comparative amounts of time Byron spent in Switzerland, Italy and Greece. The time between Byron leaving England and his death worked out neatly to around eight years, or ninety-six months. If I did a day for every month in each of his locations, it would work out perfectly as a three-month itinerary. Lucky for me, he spent

most of his time in Italy. But like they did for Byron, each
of those three countries provided sweet inspiration for the
stanzas in my ode to self.

I

Leaving

Once more upon the water! Yet once more!
And the waves bound beneath me as a steed
That knows his rider. Welcome to their roar!
Swift be their guidance, wheresoe'er it lead!

Childe Harold's Pilgrimage, Canto III

Standing on the deck of a creaking ship, his cloak waving in the wind, the sea spraying his divinely handsome face: heroic, majestic, magnificent. That's *my* image of Lord Byron as he sails from England for the final time. But other than the fact that he wrote the first three stanzas of one of his most famous works on that voyage, the biographers of Lord Byron note little more than that he was seasick. Nearly 200 years on, that speaks to the rock star he was, the original celebrity about whom such mundane details are fascinating.

Even some of the most respected literary critics have noted Lord Byron's tendency to grow fat. You could be reading about some Hollywood starlet in a trashy magazine instead of one of the greatest poets of the English language and a towering figure of Romanticism. Like Britney Spears, Lord Byron fought with one of the most basic of human frailties, and perhaps the greatest source of modern Western insecurity—the battle of the bulge. And though he penned a plethora of outstanding verse, the critics still chose to note it. Lord Byron might have been brilliant, but like Britney, just like you and me, pasta went straight to his midriff.

Smart, funny, good looking, troubled, scandalous, sexually *comme ci comme ça* and a guy who would have been featured in the celebrity diets issue of *People* magazine, had he been alive today—that was Lord Byron.

I think much of the poet's enduring attraction is how he was celebrity and artist in equal measure. For me, though, his greatest allure is how he was absolutely courageous when expressing both those parts of himself. That's why I like the lines that *he* wrote about beginning his journey to Europe and into a new life chapter, because they speak to that courage. Though he's leaving England because scandal has driven him away, though nausea might buckle him, he stands straight again, defiant and brave, invoking the ocean as if it were God or fate itself and the voyage the divine plan. Bring it on, he is saying. I'm up for whatever life throws at me from here on. The sixteen-hour crossing from England to Brussels may have been short and stomach churning, but for him it was a voyage into the unknown and immensely portentous.

One thing Byron did know for sure then was the power of travel, how it could shape a life. But he did not know how his own was to be changed. It had already been transformed profoundly and irreversibly by travel, seven years earlier, when he went on his first adventures. Like most young British men of means did as a rite of passage after they finished university, he had gone on the so-called Grand Tour after completing Cambridge. It was an interlude of months, years even, designed to give these heirs and noblemen experience of antiquities and art, culture and language. Byron's gave him that, and a great deal more.

George Gordon, Lord Byron, to give him his full title, was all of twenty-one when he embarked on that first taste of travel. It was 2 July 1809 and he set sail from England's white cliffs for Lisbon, going to Iberia and Greece, not usually on the Grand Tour itinerary, but because much of the rest of the usual European travel map—France, Germany, etc.—was at war thanks to that other big personality of the Romantic age, Napoleon. Travel became the grist for Byron's mill. He wrote the first two cantos of *Childe Harold's Pilgrimage*, one of his most lauded works. Though he insisted it was fiction, and though there was much of a fable in it, it was undeniably also his travel memoir in rhyme, recording, with instinctive poetic licence, his experiences, thoughts and the times through which he fared. He wrote its various stages progressively as he clocked up the miles.

When it was published it became the sensation that rendered him a superstar. 'I awoke one morning and found myself famous,' he said of it. Suddenly, as suddenly as his statement suggests, it turned the twenty-something nobleman into the first, original rock star. Forget Elvis, the Beatles; Byron was the prototype for modern-style fame. He became arguably the world's very first celebrity: sexy, provocative, groundbreaking, enigmatic, causing hysteria wherever he went. The young handsome poet who made lovers of both sexes blither, who caused actual swoons when he walked into rooms, whose looks, charm and charisma shone like an angel among mortals, whose audacious lack of a filter between his thoughts and social acceptability caused titillation, even shock, whenever he opened his mouth, was the most sought-after parlour guest in London and the most talked-about too.

So when he fell, he fell spectacularly. If he was once an angel among men, then he was Lucifer, his descent as dramatic as the descent of God's one-time brightest. According to the tattle-tales, hypocrites, gossips and predators who had clamoured for a piece of Byron's fame, and who now bayed for every last drop of his blood, he had become the devil himself.

Byron was said to have had an affair with his half-sister and fathered a child to her. He was rumoured to have made love to men. All that was put up with to some degree. But the thing that drove him out of England was society's whispers behind their hands that he was a sodomite and had forced the young wife who had very recently borne him a daughter to do the unspeakable—leave him. Sodomy then was a hanging offence. An unholy, unnatural act. Leaving a marriage? Beyond reckoning.

The intensity of the vitriol at these transgressions—the very public split, the rumoured sexual act against her—drove him into self-imposed exile. In April 1816 he sailed away, still only twenty-eight as he set off for the second time. But he did not go with his (allegedly pointy red) tail between his legs. Though desolate over loss of family, friends and the familiar, he left with the spirit of the undefeatable, riding those waves triumphantly like a steed towards his fate, whatever it might be. It was a fate that would see him never return home. Though he always spoke of eventually going back, he would die without doing so, eight years after the voyage on which he greeted the ocean so vehemently. But on those travels, in those final chapters of his short life, he would create a body of work, moreover an existence, that would come to exemplify what it means to be authentic. Flawed, absolutely. Self-centred, undeniably. Indulgent, quite. Unbowed, fully expressed, utterly himself, yes, yes and yes again.

*

I wouldn't have said my women friends who were married with young children were all unhappy. But I could have said that of late, each, virtually without exception, had looked at me and said, 'You're so lucky.' For most of my forties I, as a single, childless woman, had found that view of my life patronising and insensitive. But I was beginning to think maybe they were right.

Here I was, living in a sunny little apartment by the beach, decorated the way I liked, with the TV remotes tucked away into a neat little silver box. That box some of my friends found a bit neurotic but I thought it was perfect when I found it at a market and I didn't have to consult anyone about it when I installed it on my coffee table. When the remotes were allowed out of that perfect little silver box, I had full control of them. My duvet had unapologetically girly roses on it sometimes, other times more masculine chambray blue and white stripes; it depended on my mood and mine alone. I got to use the whole thing, scrunch it up under me, push it to one side, tuck it around me, while sleeping on whatever side of the bed I fancied, starfish in the middle if I so desired. I ate what I liked, slept when I liked, walked naked about the place whenever I felt like it (hello, neighbours across the way), listened to my music, from AC/DC to Mozart, without needing to gauge the mood of the crowd. I did not need to pick up anyone's stuff but mine.

And I got to travel. Lots. I'd been a journalist and writer for over twenty years. That career had already taken me to some amazing places, from living in Los Angeles to the outback. But travel writing had opened the whole world to me, and it is true to say, it had opened me up. I had come to value travel not only for showing me who other people were, but also for the way it showed me who I was. And so I upped and left any time something was on offer, which was regularly, and I did so without needing to organise a damn thing. I left no one in the lurch, no child cried when I departed, no duties needed be reorganised, nothing, no one but me needed to be considered.

I didn't see that my married friends were unlucky, though. In the absence of children and a partner there was always loneliness. I'd be tootling along completely fine, then, out of nowhere, it would slap me down. I'd been so lonely across my single years. But in being a largely independent unit, perhaps there was a gift: the gift of space to become more me. I thought marriage and kids seemed a wonderful path to becoming more one's self, I sincerely did. Through family and companionship I thought I could learn a lot. But maybe one of these paths was no better than the other. They were merely different. Very different, but no better.

Well, maybe. There was a place somewhere inside me where I was unconvinced about this. But what I did know was I had once seen my unmarried, no-kids life as less of a journey, very much a destination: I am single, unmarried, childless. And I can be no more. And I knew married women who were similarly stuck: I am mother, wife, mortgage payer. End of story.

I was beginning to see it differently. I had found myself occasionally okay with my singledom. Accepting? I would get there, eventually. But back then when I was newly opening to the possibilities in it? Let's just say okay. And from that okay was springing a curiosity for what was next.

My heart desired love, companionship and children in my life (maybe; they would probably need to be someone else's) but I was also wondering: what if that was not on the cards for me? What if I was to be single for the rest of my life? I had spent a lot of time and energy bemoaning what wasn't, wishing I woke up on Sunday mornings to a loving husband, a couple of happy kids, a dog and a big sunny house, instead of alone in my apartment followed by breakfast and the papers by myself at a local café. Would I spend the next forty years (God willing) lamenting that, wishing for something other than what I had while not appreciating that which was in front of me? What an awful thought.

Maybe I needed to embrace this. Perhaps celebrating the gift of my situation, honouring it, might be the way to the fulfilment I had been wishing for.

I wanted to grasp my freedom. I wanted to live it to its fullest. I wanted to fill it with beauty and art, literature, spirituality and culture, the things that had once made my heart sing: the things I loved as a kid.

Had I given up on love? No. But I needed to stop waiting for it. I needed to get on with it.

My favourite moments in my life so far, my happiest memories, always involved no one else but Mum and me: my feisty, energy ball of a mum, whose light was snuffed out way too young. She was sixty-nine, I was thirty-two when she had a massive heart attack with no one around to call paramedics. She was here, then she wasn't. I missed her every day. So for the youngest child of a brood of six brought up by a woman who did the parenting singlehandedly and who died when I was only just into my thirties, those memories of 'her and me' times were precious.

The most precious of all involved the two of us and the collection of old, leatherbound books, the one thing in the small, damp, falling-down home at number ten Lavender Street, Ringwood, Victoria, where I grew up that I considered worth anything. I particularly liked the poetry books. These were what Mum and I shared. I was in early high school and taking a keen interest in poetry and we read Browning and we read Shelley and we read Byron, when no one else, none of my five brothers and sisters, was there. I loved those times, Mum and me by the heater, in the evening, me reading out loud, her in her dressing gown doing her crossword puzzle in her chair in the corner, the warm glow of her reading lamp over her shoulder, her head tilted just so for her bifocals.

I discovered I loved Byron. I liked that he was funny, a bit naughty sometimes. Mum said he had a clubfoot. She said he was good looking, but a bit difficult, probably because of that foot. I had an image of him in my head as something like a faun, a man with a hoof for a foot: something that looked like the end of a golf club wood from the ankle down.

Mum always said she thought Shelley a superior poet to Byron but she knew a lot about Byron anyway. I always thought of him as the poet with that clubfoot. I loved the vividness of Byron, his floridness. Where Shelley was controlled, with light brush strokes of evocative detail, Byron was all splashes of vibrant metaphor—about as subtle as my heart-on-sleeve self. He also seemed more human to me than those lofty geniuses who lined the shelves of my childhood home: Wordsworth, Browning, Shakespeare of course. Byron was damaged. He had a clubfoot.

I had spent a lot of my life feeling damaged.

I put aside my love of Romantic poetry when I left university and took up the decidedly unromantic occupation of journalist. It went by the wayside with a lot of the things I loved, including aspects of my spirituality, especially as I secretly had a decidedly uncool-in-my-circles love of the Christ energy, something that had come to the fore in my teenage years, but which I had pushed well and truly down. 'God-bothering' this was sometimes called with journalistic cynicism. I loved journalism, but I changed to survive in it. Even then, my spirituality had proven irrepressible and those closest to me, very close, knew of this side of me. Those on the newsroom floor did not. I explored a lot of different angles on spirituality but none fitted quite right until my first trip to Italy. It was by going into Italy's majestic churches, and finding myself moved by the genius of Renaissance religious art, that I found this amazing lost aspect of myself: my connection to the Christ energy. This fallen Catholic who hated so many things about the church suddenly discovered she was deeply moved by the compassion of Christ.

It was (and still is) awkward for me to say that publicly, so deep does my fear of what people might think of that run. It's so okay to say you have an Indian guru, or you dig the Buddha. But such travesties have been carried out in the name of Christ, the most loving and peaceful man who ever lived, that saying you love him can seem like you're saying you are an extreme right-wing war-mongering conservative. I think Christ was the original lefty myself, and his views on war are well known, but the point is that he was, I realised, intrinsic to who I was. It was not the church as an institution, certainly not Catholicism (though I began to enjoy the rituals and mysticism of mass for the first time in my life, especially the music at the cathedrals), it was not religion that moved me, but my relationship with Jesus and, through him, God. The deeply spiritual subtexts of all those paintings, by Caravaggio, Raphael, Titian and Michelangelo, that I saw for real in Italy, and the opportunity they offered to *feel* Christ in my own wordless interpretation of them rather than be told about him in a linear, dogmatic way, it was *this* that I responded to.

It was around the same time that my love of Byron began creeping back into my consciousness, turning up as references in those stories I wrote, particularly about Italy. They would appear on the page, typed by my fingers, but not essentially composed by me. They came out, from somewhere in the depths of my psyche, proving as irrepressible as spirit itself. My reconnection with Byron was in tandem with my spiritual emergence. And that got me thinking: maybe there was something more than poetry in his life and work for me.

There were things about his life that spoke to the way I *wanted* to be, and how I wanted to celebrate who I was. He expressed himself with abandon and passion. He lived his truth, courting controversy and infamy in the process. And he sought inspiration and pleasure, embarking on a European adventure that led to the legend he was to become. He was reviled and revered in equal measure. But he was not unrealised.

That was something to aspire to, especially now that I knew I was ready to live as myself, unfiltered. I desired to be me, unedited. I thought I could learn a thing or two from Byron. I wondered if following Byron's odyssey through Europe might be the way to celebrate who I was, who I was becoming. At the very least, it would be quite a trip.

I was an experienced traveller. I should have known the universe's idea of celebration of self and mine might be a bit different. I should have known I was invoking God, the universe, the waves of fate, inviting them to bring it on. But as I organised my itinerary, I had images of me in a convertible, scarf trailing joyously, driving the roads of Italy, men calling out '*Ciao bella!*' everywhere I went, little figuring that the reality would prove to be something a wee bit more intense.

2

Family Influence

Stern death forbade my orphan youth to share
The tender guidance of a father's care.
Can rank or even a guardian's name supply
The love that glistens in a father's eye?

Childish Recollections

Though we forge our own way in life, the path we begin down is carved by our times, circumstance and family. For George Gordon, Lord Byron, historic nobility dictated circumstance. The first Byron arrived in England from Normandy as a follower of William the Conqueror.

Family would bestow something decidedly less noble. Within a mere handful of generations the crazy factor would emerge. The first to show it, in the annals anyway, would be the 'Wicked Lord', the poet's great-uncle, who got his nickname for his libertine and murderous ways, depression and episodes of insanity that plagued him as he plunged into debt so deep he leased or sold off the family's most valuable assets.

His nephew, John Byron, the father of the poet, was equally troubled. Known as 'Mad Jack', he was sent to military school near Paris, where he sold his services rent-boy style after his folks cut him off for his waywardness. Back in England at twenty-two, he had a torrid affair with a rich married aristocrat, ran back to France with her and parented Augusta, George Gordon's half-sister. When his scarlet lady died, Mad Jack went searching for a rich wife. He found one in England, in the chubby, socially awkward twenty-year-old, Catherine Gordon of Gight.

What a match. She too had a family history full of depression, suicides and other tragedy. When Catherine fell pregnant they were living barely ahead of debtors' jail; Jack's outrageous lifestyle had dwindled what Catherine had, which wasn't as much as Jack had at first thought, anyway. So with bailiffs on his tail, Jack left her, and ran to France again, where he lived with his sister and his little daughter.

Catherine took a humble room in London and gave birth to a baby boy with a lame foot, George Gordon Byron, right at the time when Napoleon was tearing up Europe, defining the age in which the young man would mature with a heightened sense of war, politics, idealism and, in the end, disillusionment. Destitute from Jack's leeching and Catherine's weakness, mother and son would be forced to move back to Aberdeen, Catherine's ancestral home, and rely on the kindness of outsiders and extended family to keep a roof over their heads and food in their stomachs, a strange and awkward situation for people of noble lineage. Jack would seek them out now and then to harass money out of his wife. But the three would seldom live as a family again, although enough for the poet to claim early recollections of two people, his parents, screaming at each other on these random opportunities.

Jack died in August 1791, when his little boy was not yet three. The paternal absence would leave an imaginative son free to romanticise his roguish dad. And the paternal ideal would also bond him to his half-sister Augusta, with whom he eventually would have a sexual relationship. He would always claim her his one true love, the only woman to understand him, the split of the same soul. That relationship would emerge in drawing-room whispers and contribute to his self-exile.

In May 1798, seven years after his father's death, George Gordon inherited the title of Lord Byron thanks to the paternal side of the family having no heirs between him and the Wicked Lord. Life for George Gordon, only ten years old, changed.

Society viewed him one way, while the reality of his life was something quite different. He and his mother were only farthings away from poverty most of the time. His mother, admittedly stressed as a single parent, and under siege from the everyday expense of bringing up a lord, was hysterical, manipulative, at times mean and obsessed with her son. The estate he inherited, Newstead in Sherwood Forest, had been denuded of assets and the house had been let go to a Gothic shambles. In the Nottingham society to which he was introduced he was noted as a bright, witty boy. Behind closed doors, Lord Byron's lush of a nanny was abusing him, beating him one minute, sexually interfering with him the next.

And so the young, brilliant man grows up to fear intimacy. He's sexually dysfunctional, taking on lovers like others take showers. He's angry at the system into which he is born, dismissive of the parlours that idolise him, shamed by his deformed leg and lethal in the use of his overcompensating cache of charms. What classic self-loathing, an open-and-shut case for a psychiatrist, and that will be one hundred and fifty dollars, thank you very much.

There seems monumental disconnection from self in that story, yet there's breathtaking honesty in his writing—not only his poetry, but his letters too. He saw much and felt deeply. He lived a life unedited, a big, flawed, full-tilt life, despite all the pain and dysfunction.

And perhaps he would not have done that, had he lived in an age when psychiatry would have prevented Napoleon and a bunch of mad, wicked relatives being the pointer in his hand of fate. There's something to be said for exorcising one's demons through art. As long as the exorcism works and the powerful combination of demons and art does not consume their host alive.

I spent the twenty-odd years between my parents divorcing and me first going to see a therapist absolutely believing I had not been affected at all by events in my childhood. For instance, as a twenty-something I would say when the opportunity arose, 'I wasn't affected at all by Mum and Dad's divorce. Erin was, but I wasn't,' referring to the sister just a bit older than me. I honestly thought I was this perfectly well-adjusted, above-it-all creature. I did. It was hilarious, now I think about it.

I was in my mid-thirties when a psychologist pointed out that my childhood was quite awful. It was a rude shock. I walked out of her practice in the inner east of Sydney feeling like someone had dynamited the foundations out from under my house of self. Every single thing I believed about me was null and void. Every single premise upon which I had built a life, the way I defined myself, all was gone.

I had visited her after my relationship of the better part of a decade had broken up. I had recently returned after being in Los Angeles for two years, where I had lived a crazy, exciting, busy life as a foreign correspondent. My mother had died only in the past few years and I had been feeling unhappy. Just unhappy. That was all. And I just wanted to feel happy again. Instead, I was dismantled.

I didn't go back to that psychologist, and to her credit, she did ring me a few times to try and get me to. But she had frightened me beyond that which I was equipped to handle. I did not feel safe with her. I think she was very new to the game, though I didn't know that then. The way she told me point blank that my life was a lie, and whoops, time's up, there's the door, was naïve, to be kind about it.

It was around this time that I began drinking heavily alone. I'm not blaming her, the therapist, for that. It was probably coming anyway, in some form or another. And she was right; I did need to get past that whole Miss Well-adjusted 1998 thing I had going on and face up to all the stuff it was covering up. But it would take me another ten years to do that. Another ten years of drinking that took hold and shook me, like a crazed dog does its prey. Lucky for me, a hand would come down and pull me from those jaws in the nick of time.

It was astonishing when it did, at the beginning of 2008. Suddenly, I mean really out of the blue, I wanted to quit drinking. One minute I had absolutely no power over alcohol. The next, I did. The catalyst: a terrible hangover from what was actually a good night during which I had not been drinking by myself but with others at a dinner party. And I'd enjoyed myself. But there was something about this hangover, an energy in the self-berating that had life change on a pinhead.

I had been to that precipice before. I had promised myself all kinds of things on many a morning, and yet, come five or six o'clock in the evening of the very same day, I would find myself buying a bottle of wine. I would quieten the misery of losing to liquor's lure with the first sip, and then annihilate it for the night, with the tipsy fantasy that a life lived drinking expensive wine out of an expensive glass was a life lived well.

This was entirely different. There were no ifs or buts. In

a flash I had the clarity to see that I was faced with a critical either/or situation. Keep going the way I was going, choosing alcohol as my comfort and friend, and die a living death. Or choose an undefined something different. I didn't know what I was choosing by choosing to say 'enough' but I knew I could no longer deny the grave spiritual, emotional and physical danger that I had been courting. Here I was at a turning point, a moment of truth. Life or death: that was the choice. This drinking compulsion, it was not who I really was. I saw that, and in the time it takes to move from one moment to the next, I had put one foot on the path to recovery and, hey, look at that— it was a moving walkway. A momentum beyond my control began to steer me away from the mindless misery into which I had been descending.

I gave up drinking completely for eighteen months, toying with the idea that I might have been alcoholic. Toying, I say, but I never did anything more serious in my life. I went to AA meetings, read all the amazing literature, before I realised the fellowship, though wonderful and powerful and a miracle, was not for me. But that was not before AA recommenced the excavation job that had been started by that psychologist's wayward stick of dynamite.

I was born the last of six children and grew up in a small weatherboard house in what was orchard land, now suburban sprawl, in the outer east of Melbourne. That house was built over a filled-in creek with nothing between the floorboards and the dirt that blocked that waterway but a tract of musty, damp space we called 'under the house'. Cats would have kittens under there. We'd hear them mewing, then my father would do something. And no more mewing. We had strange, often darkly dramatic, but also fun times in that house, though I knew as soon as I knew anything that things were falling apart:

the house, our frayed old towels, my parents' relationship.

I chose to not fall apart in any way. Hold my breath. Play nice. But everyone around me was barely coping. I could see it. If only I was like this, or like that, then I wouldn't cause these people trouble. Those people were my siblings, the two boys fifteen and fourteen years older than me, the sister twelve years my elder, who was a teenager but had to take some care of us younger kids. Then two little girls—me, my sister Erin, nearly three years older than me—and another boy six years older. And Mum, of course. Dad caused her enough grief. She didn't need it from me.

This is actually painting an inaccurate picture, though. I tried to not cause trouble, but I was terrible at it. I was always falling out of trees, falling off things, cutting my knees open, banging myself about. And as I got older, more rubbish would spill over and out. I couldn't keep a lid on life, ever. Drama began to follow me, despite my best efforts to run from it. I seemed to run into it, more than away.

I had passed six months without a drink in late 2008 when I stopped running. When I turned for the first time and faced the marauding throng of emotions that had been chasing me for years and years. I had no intention of doing so. I was at my job at Fairfax newspapers like any other day, when management announced via email that there was to be large-scale retrenchment. The whole place went into a panic. The big immediate outrage among staff was over a perception that management had moved without consultation. No consultation was happening post the announcement, either. They had their reasons, I'm sure. But I was on deadline, editing a large feature section for the Sunday paper, and had no choice but to keep going with what I was doing.

I was sitting at my desk, looking at my screen, and then I wasn't. I had fallen into a hole. The world went black, all I heard was my ears ringing, and with an aching pang I wanted to drink. I came back to the world, petrified and just so sad. The immensity of the moment was threatening to swallow me.

A few days later, I was sitting in a women-only AA gathering at the Bondi Junction Crypt, where I'd gone to my first ever meeting. I was listening to a woman share a story of childhood misery when a box, marked 'Do Not Disturb', packed away in a dark recess of my subconscious, came into view and sprang open. It was this box that had been lurking down the bottom of that tunnel. It was what was in it that had made me black out then want to drink. In that box was the frozen moment in time when I decided that my needs and emotions would never matter, that the needs and emotions of others would always override them.

Inside was me, a child of about three, lying in bed listening to my parents scream at each other, my father drunk, moving back and forth between caustic and sharp, laughing and derogatory. And my mother at the height of a focused murderous mania vomiting out the contents of a poisoned heart. It was loud and relentless and oblivious to the other people in that small, damp house. If any pretence of civility had been left between them, it was gone that night.

Erin slept on in the bunk above me. I could hear her lightly snore. One of the boys suddenly yelled from the room next door, 'Stop it, stop it, stop it, stop it!'

I don't remember it stopping. But it must have and the sun must have come up the next day. To my recollection, no one ever spoke about that night. We never did speak of such things. We moved on and got on with it. And I filed it away, very securely indeed.

It is a difficult concept for me, the one of soul contracts and of choosing our experience. If I chose the parents I had, I also chose to be that traumatised child who shut that night away and then began an epic marathon of running to keep from releasing it. I had long known there was something unacknowledged in the shadows, some moment at which an important part of my ability to function had been damaged. When it welled up at AA that day, after I got over my amazement at the ability of the human mind to block out something so resolutely and for so long, I was a bit disappointed. Was that it? No abuse like Lord Byron had endured? Not that I was wishing that upon myself. It was just that a blue between my parents, albeit a raging, foul, bile-spitting hate fest, was not exactly Charles Dickens.

The feeling of insignificance and powerlessness I felt then though was a big one. I sensed other people feeling that, there in the newspaper office on that day when the retrenchments were announced, and it triggered the memory of the original time when I felt my needs didn't matter.

And the drinking? Why did I want to drink in that moment? The same reason I ate too much as a kid and, sadly, ate too much until the end of that year of not drinking. To push it all down.

I used to be terrified of hunger. It took twelve months of not drinking to let me see that. I ate huge dinners. Healthy food, mostly. But lots of it. Being full to distended was one of my chosen anaesthetics.

I reached a point where I didn't want to be anaesthetised any more. Spirit had found a way through, and it felt so good I wanted to clear a path for it. And so my eating changed. I lost eleven kilos in six months. It was a spiritual manifestation, no question.

I did think then that I had it all sorted. That I was healed, cured, complete, had entered happily ever after ... and numerous other fallacies. Where I actually was, was at the very beginning of re-emergence and I had a long road in front of me. Travelling it would reveal a mosaic of reasons for why I drank the way I drank: that therapist, my parents' divorce, their vile argument, but more besides. And there would be a centrepiece to it, a surprising to me, completely buried centrepiece, which, like that box springing open, would come to light when I least expected it.

3

Geneva

Fare thee well!—thus disunited—
Torn from every nearer tie—
Seared in heart—and lone—and blighted—
More than this, I scarce can die.

Fare Thee Well!

At the end of March 1812, Lord Byron was at the height of his social cachet in London. Women went into conniptions when he walked into rooms. Men were entranced. He was a tall, long-necked, luscious-locked, pouty-lipped, gorgeous creature with big heavy-lidded eyes, alabaster skin, and the standoffish aloofness women so love combined with a praeternatural social charm when he chose to turn it on. And of course, a sexual energy that radiated. In uptight English society, he was a beacon of desire and desirability.

But his kind of fame, the celebrity kind, had brought to him what it always does: infamy. And though he clearly enjoyed the attention, it did also trouble him. He took his peerage and his poetry very seriously and, like every modern artist who has become a source of fascination as much for their personal myth as for their art, he wanted to be taken as seriously as he took himself.

He had been entangled with Lady Caroline Lamb. A married society figure with a wild streak, she would turn something of a stalker when Byron broke it off. She spread tawdry stories about him but she coined the most famous, and wonderful, of all descriptions of Byron: 'Mad, bad and dangerous to know.'

Annabella Milbanke was Caroline's cousin from the country, religious, academic, moralistic and disapproving—Caroline's polar opposite. Self-sacrificing Annabella, in London to be at the bedside of a sick friend, accepted an invitation to Lady Caroline's Easter party, even though she was vocal in her disdain for society and its participants. It was there she met Lord Byron.

In letters between Annabella and Lord Byron it's clear that there was an intellectual connection. But Lord Byron had reached one of those junctures in his life at which human beings do something because they think they ought, not because it resonates as truly right for them on a soul level. Enough with the married ladies, the young men, the swooners and strumpets. It was time to take a wife. He married Annabella. It was inevitable that for someone as passionate as Byron, 'the right thing' would be so very much the wrong. It would have life-altering consequences.

Society was all a-chatter about his sexual cruelty to her. There's no excusing brutishness, but living a lie can make beasts of angels, and Lord Byron was no angel. Annabella was a handful herself, not the most stable of human beings, but she was dealing with another deception: Byron's affair with Augusta Leigh, his half-sister, allegedly continued during their marriage. Given that, these days it wouldn't be surprising that a year after marrying him and having borne him a daughter, Ada, Annabella left Byron. But it was a drastic move for the time. And it was the scandal ensuing from her leaving that drove Lord Byron into self-imposed exile.

We die to ourselves at times in our lives, attempting to live as something we are not. I like to think there is a point to these deaths: to resurrect a better version, become truer to ourselves by facing up to that which we are not, and so become closer to who we really are, an expression of God's loveliness. They can be painful, drawn-out episodes, though. And some of us never make it through to resurrection. We walk through the rest of life in a spiritual death state.

My trip to Geneva was via Singapore Airlines A380 to London. Business class. I was perched in a ridiculously big leather seat, with gorgeous flight attendants acting as if I was the most important person in the world. There was yummy food and lots of sleep. This did little to correct my misguided notion that I'd entered happily ever after. Then I took the Eurostar from London to Paris and felt exactly like a rock star. Was that Anna Wintour in the row up ahead? I boarded one of those super-fast trains from Paris to Geneva and felt more international than I ever have before when, at Paris Gare du Nord, I saw a formidable-looking African gent and, following him, a large, worried-looking bodyguard, an assistant in a strange bottle-green suit, a wife in a long flowing caftan and veil, and a trolley full of Louis Vuitton luggage. They got on my carriage and I tried to resist staring. I was unsuccessful. It's a wonder the bodyguard didn't move me on.

But I soon had other things to look at when we entered the French countryside. At Mâcon Loché station I saw a young couple kissing passionately as if their lives depended on it, the black and white poster cliché. A woman carrying a perfect bunch of lilies of the valley, their stalks wrapped in tin foil, walked by them, looking this way and that for the person for whom the bouquet was intended. It was all so charming and I was duly charmed.

I pulled one of my Byron books out of my bag to make use of the travel time, like all the laptop-clacking diplomats around me. But I caught a glimpse of contented woolly sheep resting by a brook down the hill from a ramshackle stone farmhouse and I pressed my nose to the window again. In green, green pastures, fat, glossy cows in small groups looked for all the world like the happy cow on Laughing Cow cheese packets. I saw donkeys, hedgerows, paths begging to be followed into woodland. We streamed by fly fishermen thigh deep in excitable rivers. There were fruit trees in full blossom and the sun sent silver glitter down onto them. There were clusters of alpine wildflowers and irises growing by the side of the train tracks at Culoz.

Why would anyone fly across this?

It was curious to be in Geneva, Lord Byron's first port of call on his exile. For me too, it was the city that had signified the beginning of my own, unconscious attempts at self-exile.

In my two decades as a journalist, I had covered an eerie murder of a tiny American child beauty queen, a mass shooting, even a mass suicide. I'd covered bush fires and all manner of misery. But nothing prepared me for flying to Indonesia on New Year's Eve 2004, five days after a massive tsunami, when the world was beginning to realise that the country's northern province of Aceh was the place hit hardest by the disaster. The afternoon before I left, the man I had only recently finally broken up with after several years of on–off mayhem popped over to my place to say, I'm not sure what: happy new year, bon voyage, hope you don't get typhoid? There was nothing appropriate to say. The man was the man I was in love with, my heart was ripped to shreds and, on top of that, I was scared like I never had been before.

I had become adept at not showing the depths of my pain. So when he asked me to drive him in his car up to the shops and cruise around the block while he did the banking for his small business, saying, 'It will be impossible to get a park up there on New Year's Eve,' I had no one to blame but myself. I carried out the errand, and on the third lap of the block as I waited for him, asked myself why. When he got out of the passenger seat at my place, promptly replaced me at the wheel and left without so much as a 'May I drive you to the airport on the hardest afternoon of the year to get a taxi?', that 'why' had been replaced by a 'Why, for God's sake, woman, why?'

I bought at an airport newsstand *He's Just Not That Into You* and read the entire thing on the plane to Jakarta. But it did no good. There was always something that stood invisibly between me and the way things should be. It was a wonder I was ever surprised that things did not turn out the way they seemed to for other people.

Arriving in Jakarta minutes after midnight, 1 January 2005, the dark streets around Jalan Jaksa, the city's backpacker strip where my hotel was, were overtaken by a cavalry of tandem motorbike riders blowing plastic horns. I heard them as mournful, not celebratory. I knew it was over with the man. The sadness of the realisation completely obliterated any nervousness I might have had regarding the horror I was about to witness. Thousands had died. My heart had been broken again. I was not the first human to let romance rule my sense of perspective.

But I was nothing if not hopeful. On New Year's Day, I met up with the American photographer who was on the assignment with me and we made our way to the airport. We were in the check-in queue when I heard the voice first. 'Steven, how you doing?' it said to the photographer.

'Jim, long time,' Steven replied. I turned around to look at Jim.

'Wasn't the last time Sierra Leone?' this international journalist, Jim, said. I fell for him on the spot.

Tall, geeky, bespectacled yet manly, with gravitas to him I longed to have myself, he became my focus for the entire week I was amid the rubble, bodies, mud, death and chaos. I did my job. But my infatuation kept me detached from it.

When I came back, I told the man I'd met somebody. That felt good, but sad also. I took the good and left the sad somewhere; I knew not the exact spot. Jim had not the faintest idea it was him whom I had met but I felt sure that one day ... I kept the dream up, emailing him with bright, witty, look-at-me tap dances and put him front and centre of my visualisations. And he was ... polite, not particularly revealing in his communications, but communicative.

I was drinking a bottle of wine a night then. I could not resist buying some expensive drop on the way home from work. It had to be expensive and my glassware was too. I did not even cast a glance at any of the whys and wherefores of it. But I would come home, cook a big dinner for myself, eat till I was stuffed, drink my wine out of my expensive glass, and send application after application to Geneva, the seat of the United Nations, for gigs with its various branches: UNHCR, WHO, UNICEF ... I covered the alphabet in acronyms. I applied for other jobs at NGOs such as the Red Cross, most of them headquartered in Geneva, believing all my problems would be solved if I could only find a worthy engagement.

Then in February 2005, I had not got so much as a 'your application has been unsuccessful' back from all my job correspondence when the first episode of the TV show *LOST* aired in Australia. I sat down with my vino to watch. In the first two minutes there was a shot of a dead body wedged in the top of a palm tree. That was the thing about self-medication. Sometimes I got it wrong. Instead of the numbing effect I was hoping to get from the television and wine combo, that new show suddenly had Aceh belting back at me. All the uncontrollability, the helplessness, the unfairness of it, the deep, unreachable sadness of the tsunami aftermath, this crashed over me like the water that had caused it. But it was of course the uncontrollability, the helplessness, the deep sadness within myself that caught up to me then. Unexpectedly, irrevocably, I was reduced to a flood of grief. Then a chasm seemed to open up in the middle of the water. It felt like it sucked me further down than the bottom, into some subterranean void.

I almost lost consciousness. It was impossible to breathe. But the next day, I stopped drinking for the first time.

When I was approached not long after to start a magazine for young women, I fell hook, line and sinker for the image of myself as a big shot editor. When they mentioned the pay, the post-tsunami need to do something meaningful with my life and help people went out the window. Sort of. I allowed myself to be convinced that doing a magazine for young women could be my equivalent of working for an NGO. I could make a difference to the ideas- and inspiration-starved. I would be more use here than writing press releases for a charity. Young affluent Western women were as much in need of rescue—a different, bourgeois kind of rescue, but who was I to judge?

I was uneasy about it initially. I'd been doing a course on manifesting my heart's desire. I'd been visualising myself living in Bangkok, the hub of South-East Asian media, shacked up with an important, rugged international type (read, Jim, who lived in the Big Mango), spending my days fighting the good fight for the UNHCR and my evenings penning an expat epic, the likes of which would not have been seen since Graham Greene's body of work. Editing a chick mag in Sydney was about as far removed from that as my short fair looks are from Angelina Jolie's lithe darkness.

But perhaps this was a stepping-stone to that destiny? Who was I to fight that which the universe intended? Someone told me my unease with the offer was fear of success. I had sweated throughout the initial interview, so heavily that a torrent ran down my back, and it was the middle of winter. I was glad I was wearing black.

I found myself agreeing to the magazine project. And six months into it, when I had to sack someone, I started drinking again. I worked hard on the magazine by day, then would go home and drink a bottle of red wine before crying myself to sleep. I would get up early, go to the gym, work a long day like a mad woman ... and repeat.

Cut to me standing in a big designer office presenting mock-ups to a potential advertiser, a man wearing a nice suit. Things at the magazine were as normal, that is, borderline tolerable, until the man said, 'I love how Paris touches herself', as if it was a perfectly fine observation to make in front of me.

You have four choices at a time like this. You can roll with it. You can buy into it. You can go into meltdown. Choice four is that voice inside your head which guides you away, saying, *This is not who you really are. This is not who you really are.* And you can listen to that voice, pull out and move on.

The cover of the mock-up *did* feature a picture of Paris Hilton, dancing with her hand poised artfully over the area in which her pubic hair would have been were she not a publicly proven fan of the Brazilian. And I hated myself for being there. This was not why I had become a journalist. As soon as you inject a situation with the intensity of passion I felt at that moment, you can bet your life the universe is going to move. Move it did.

It left me jobless. Cashed up—thank you—as a result of my danger money, highly paid contract being paid out, but jobless. And wondering how life came to this, how a person with the prospects I had, the dreams I had, the chances I had, ended up like this. I might have been cashed up, but I was also humiliated. Embarrassed, ashamed, full of self-loathing at my failure and oh so humiliated. There'd been a massive hoopla of publicity about me taking on that magazine. I was a published author working for a then-reputable feature magazine. I was a journalist with a not-too-shabby reputation of her own, who had only months before been on assignment in Banda Aceh.

But now it had ended. Somehow, we'd got to the point where what I had set out to do was not what they wanted. The result was predictable. I should have seen it coming. On the Sunday after that first issue came out, I got back from the beach to find the CEO had sent me a text message, calling me into the office for a meeting. At that meeting he told me that he was bringing in an editor-in-chief above me. I wasn't sacked, just superseded.

I cried. Cried and cried and cried. 'You knew who I was when you hired me,' I implored between sobs. 'You came after me when I said no. This is not fair. You knew who you were getting!' I whined as snot streamed. I actually don't think the poor man did know who he was getting. Because I don't think I did. We came to an arrangement. I listened to that voice inside my head. I did not go back to that magazine.

A week later I was reading another magazine that had a feature on Italy in it. Not twenty minutes later, I was at a travel agent and buying a ticket to Rome. It was on that trip that I first tried my hand at travel writing, and it was on that trip that my love of Italy was forged—and my reconnection to Byron began.

4

Lac Leman

My very chains and I grew friends,
So much a long communion tends
To make up what we are:—even I
Regain'd my freedom with a sigh.

The Prisoner of Chillon

It was in Geneva that Lord Byron met fellow poet Percy Bysshe Shelley and his partner, the great Gothic novelist Mary Wollstonecraft who would become Mary Shelley. He also met Mary's half-sister, Claire Clairmont. The triumvirate of the deeply thoughtful Shelley, intellectual Mary and brilliant Lord Byron became one of the greatest legions of English literature, the union of three extraordinary young minds, bonded in ideals, cemented in tragedy. Claire, not a literary type, would shape Lord Byron's life in a different, though equally profound way. Lord Byron already had Ada, not yet two, to Annabella when he impregnated Claire that summer in Geneva.

Claire gets a bum rap from historians and biographers. She's mostly painted as a groupie, someone Byron got lumped with because of her relationship to Shelley, and because she bore him a child, and because she would climb the steep rise from the Shelleys' Geneva abode on the lake's edge to reach the bed of Lord Byron in Villa Diodati. Lord Byron himself was disdainful, saying that due to the effort she went to he could not possibly play 'the stoic'. But one biographer, Fiona McCarthy, in my favourite book about the poet, *Byron: Life and Legend*, puts forward the theory that Claire, above any, loved him unconditionally; letters from her to him clearly illustrate how ready she was to call him on his stuff, his attitudes to women, and his attitudes to anyone he might consider competition.

Whatever the case, from their union came Allegra, with whom I share the birthday 12 January—a feisty, funny little thing whose, in the end, sad story would tell much of Byron's character. Parenthood is a fount of truths from the soul.

Lord Byron would never see Ada, 'sole daughter of my house and heart' as he wrote about her, again. Hardly all Annabella's fault, given he would spend the rest of his life on the Continent, but Ada was not the only female being wrenched from his life by his estranged wife. Annabella was hard at work on the poet's half-sister Augusta, preying on her guilt and bullying her into an allegiance against Lord Byron. Few blows would have as strong an impact as the withdrawal of these female relations from his life.

I can't help but wonder about the impact his absence had on them.

There were lilacs in bloom everywhere in Geneva. They drooped heavily with fat formations of tiny dark purple, mauve and white flowers that scented the air intoxicatingly. Extraordinarily lush wisteria and the flowering tree we knew as the snowball tree at my childhood home, but which is actually called viburnum, spilled over fences and fell like confetti across pavements. Our garden contained a couple of those bushes, and us Jameson kids would pull off the soft, white, green-tinged flowers in handfuls and throw them at each other.

Those old-fashioned flowers—wisteria, lilac, viburnum— always took me back to one of those rare times in my childhood when my dad was home.

I had a strawberry-pink little dress with a full skirt and pale-pink Jiffy slippers with pink bows secured on the front of them with gold binding. We used to get Jiffy slippers for Christmas quite regularly, Erin and I, for a while there. One sunny morning I was having a good hair day, my long blonde curls yet to be butchered into an edgy 1970s dolly cut, an ugly mullet-like hairdo, severe at best and not for a child in single digits of age with a look that went to the tomboy side of female. I lost innocence with that haircut. I was, to be frank, freckly, tubby and not particularly cute. My blonde ringlets were all I had.

But still ringlet-mopped, I was at the front door with my dad, greeting some visitor. The visitor smiled at me in my pink dress and Jiffy slippers and complimented me. Smiling, my dad looked down at me and said, 'My sugarplum fairy.' It was the only time I could recall him saying anything of the kind. A beam of light pulsed through me. I went down to the lilac bush, which set off my dress and slippers rather well, I thought, and acted out long scenes with me as that mythical little sprite. I remember it so well because it was such a rare thing.

My dad's name was Ernest, named after his dad, but he went by his middle name, Bryan. He was a man's man, a somewhat deliberately styled Hemingway-type character who spear fished, went on safari and wore a shark's tooth around his neck. He smoked a pipe, drank hard and wrote. He was a journalist and he was the smartest guy I have possibly ever known, with more diverse interests than most people even attempt to ponder. He was funny and charismatic. But the suburbs weren't for him and he was a terrible dad. He'd come home from whatever jaunt he'd been on and insult neighbours, upset Mum and attempt to discipline his fast-growing-up youngest son who was used to him not being around. He'd mortify his oldest daughter with his all-out-there sexual energy, which he didn't mind exercising on any women who came across his path, including her friends or her brothers' girlfriends. He was this massive, unwieldy, unfettered, unorthodox being who should not have had six children.

He would not, could not pause his life for children. It was beyond him. The party would not be sacrificed for parenthood. Neither would the story. When on a news yarn, nothing else mattered, especially not his children. There were times when Erin and I, on weekends staying with him, would be in the car while he listened to confronting interviews on his tape recorder. Devil worshippers, seedy underworld characters, you name it, we'd be privy to it. Or we'd be in the bar when he met with dodgy contacts. Or told to wait in the car while he shored up some lead or another in a weird part of town.

But his priorities made themselves clearest to me when he used me as bait in his plan to get the goods on someone he suspected of child molestation. Stranger still, the person he suspected was a close family friend of his second wife. The way he compartmentalised his relationships, was able to distance himself and objectify people he should have had strong emotional bonds to, characterised his parental style.

For a few years after our parents divorced in the early to mid-1970s, Erin and I would go on holiday with him and his second wife at a beach house in Flinders on the Mornington Peninsula. Sometimes Damien, the second oldest boy of my family, would be there, with his guitar and harmonica, living the hippie ideal as he was, travelling with theatre groups and carving out a good career for himself as an actor and stage director.

And sometimes others would be there.

After a long, alcohol-fuelled dinner in the big dine-in kitchen at the friend's beach house, Erin, then twelve, and I were on our way to bed when Dad suggested I sleep in the living room on the mattresses on the floor with an overnight guest, this female family friend. Strangely, this was agreed to.

The lights went out around the house, and in the darkness the family friend offered me a cigarette. I told her I didn't smoke. 'Come on,' she said. 'All kids your age smoke.' I was ten. I didn't.

We were in sleeping bags. 'It's getting cold,' she said.

'Yeah,' I answered, not feeling cold at all but on edge. Timid. I never felt timid.

'We should join our sleeping bags together, then you won't get cold.'

She got out of her sleeping bag and so I got out of mine and she pushed the mattresses together then zipped the two sleeping bags together. We entered them, and I lay there uncertain.

The door was thrust open. The lights jammed on. My father, eyes blazing, chest puffed, stood accusing the woman. Things I recall him saying, then: he'd been listening the whole time, molest ...

'She said she was cold. The girl said she was cold,' the woman protested.

His relationship with my mother was combative. Based on that, I had long ago decided that if there was an opportunity to get some points against him, to get them. 'I said I was cold,' I concurred, even though I hadn't. I just wanted to contradict him.

I saw the look on his face: anger at my lack of willingness to stand as co-accuser, and then a kind of defeat. I had won.

Against the master of mind games, I had won. The woman left the room and I was left alone in that double sleeping bag, in the dark. And after a lot of yelling in the kitchen, the woman left. But no one came to talk to me. Nothing was said. That was not what we did.

For me, however, what needed to be said had already been articulated by the whole sorry episode. I already had the belief that my needs didn't matter; my dad's astonishing display was ample proof of that being bang on the money.

I took a room in a guesthouse in the Geneva suburb of Cologny where green, flower-dotted fields of plump ponies and more of those happy cows nuzzled up to the professionally tended gardens surrounding the bespoke mansions of ambassadors and old-school stars, the likes of Roger Moore, Petula Clark and Charles Aznavour. Lord Byron's residence during his summer in Switzerland was one of those mansions, a grand place that today radiates a welcoming grace. It was in this splendid, warm house of light stone with Greco-Roman columns holding up a huge, airy, sunny front terrace that Byron became firm friends with the Shelley posse and it was in this house that they amused themselves by trading horror stories, one of which would become Mary Wollstonecraft's classic Gothic novel, *Frankenstein*. Those on the Shelley trail might wish for something a tad more forbidding than the happy welcome of Villa Diodati.

I was not one of those. I decided it was my favourite house in the Cologny neighbourhood before I even realised it was what it was. I was walking in what I thought was its general direction, along a winding road lined with magnificent home after magnificent home, some behind high clipped hedges or stone walls that spilled over with fleshy roses in full fragrant bloom, others barely visible through artfully planted gardens of majestic trees. I came around a bend and saw this unhidden beauty, a low stone fence demarking her patch, blowsy rhododendrons dancing about her, the evening sun caressing her from across Lake Geneva. I saw the sign noting that the third canto of *Childe Harold's Pilgrimage* had been written here. My heart skipped.

And so I hatched this great plan to go up to the field next to Villa Diodati and read Canto III of *Childe Harold* under AVO distance away from where Lord Byron wrote it. I was sure the owners of the villa were about to get a restraining order out on me, I'd been haunting it so since I got to Geneva. But Lord Byron thought of himself as an outsider looking in, so to be in restraining order distance from the house seemed fitting.

I got up there and discovered a party was going on at the villa. The sun was out and there were catering vans at the service entrance and UN-looking types in suits and sensible heels walking down the driveway.

There is a steeply declining field next door to the Villa Diodati with perfect views of the lake. The city uses the space for special occasions, for gatherings and views of fireworks and such. But today, there was no one but a group of youths drinking beers and hanging out. And me. I scaled down the knoll to the spot in the middle of the field where there is a stone bench and from where I could see the face of Villa Diodati, the gorgeous façade of her that smiled perfectly into the Geneva sunset.

I peered up at the balcony. There were the suits, talking calmly over cocktails on that stunning terrace with its view of the lake and the UN building. I lifted my camera to take pictures; the sky was blue and the villa looked heavenly. Then I saw them. Three hawks were patrolling the field and the grounds of the villa, hungry for whatever little critters had made the snake-sized holes in the ground. The sun was brilliant on the water in front of the villa, while black clouds hung over the UN side of the lake. The rain in them produced strips of different intensity through the light. The wind was gentle through the old trees and I could see the parts of the scene that had remained unchanged. The rhythmic beauty forged by Lake Geneva's unusual topography was no doubt as dramatic and changeable when Lord Byron looked out on it and wrote down the stuff it dredged from the dark corners of his mind and soul. I could feel it doing similarly to me.

Most of the suits had their coat tails turned to all that.

I opened up my book of Lord Byron's writing. This was the first time I had read his poetry since university, some twenty-five years earlier. And quite naturally, reading it aloud seemed the right thing to do. I did think of the youths drinking beer for about a second. But only for a second.

I was good at reading poetry aloud. It was a skill I'd had ever since my early, steady diet of A.A. Milne. But I didn't hear myself reading poetry, like I had at high school, or like I had with my mum, trying to impress her with my diction and phrasing, or with Rose, the part-time lesbian and ravishingly Victorian beauty who lived up to her name, and with whom I'd had a half-hearted fling in third-year literature while on the rebound from my first boyfriend, much to the agony of a male tutor or two, and who was probably the last person to ever hear me read poetry out loud.

Maybe the youths drinking beer were hearing me, but I wasn't. I heard Lord Byron's pain. And I heard mine. And then I heard the suits'. And the youths'. And then the world's.

Empathy, when it thrusts itself on you like that, is like a microcosm in which you see all the hawks chasing all the critters, and hear all the leaves rustling in all the breezes, and see all the suits turning their backs on all the sunrays. You see time immemorial. And you see how we all feel the same kernel of a thing. We are all trying to do the best we can, at any given moment, with what we have been dealt. The bird, the critter, the youth, the suit. Me. Lord Byron. My mum. My dad. You.

Lord Byron was many a thing but he was not a man afraid to be alone with his thoughts. And he was not a man afraid to express them. This was where he had me now terrified. In this vortex of seeing his soul's connection to mine, to the people standing on his old terrace, to the hawks hovering over me, members of whose bloodline had probably done the same over Lord Byron's curl-festooned head, it struck me that I had to be as honest as he and relentlessly so. Because if I wasn't going to be, then what was I doing even thinking about following his footsteps? It was time in my life to face all my darkness, all my secrets, all my fears, because it was through so doing that I would find the peace I sought. I saw that clearly, too.

> Clear placid Leman! Thy contrasted lake,
> With the wild world I dwelt in, is a thing
> Which warns me, with its stillness, to forsake
> Earth's troubled waters for a purer spring.

I read those lines, in the third canto of *Childe Harold*, as the lake, variously known as Leman or Geneva, was painted by thick, amorphous, elephant-grey clouds and a candy-pink setting sun. I felt the truth in them.

5

Milan

We are the fools of time and terror: Days
Steal on us and steal from us; yet we live,
Loathing our life, and dreading still to die.

Manfred, Act II

He crossed the Alps from Switzerland to Italy admiring nature, and of course, the feminine wiles of the locals. He was not anonymous—the large, distinct carriage with his crest on the doors saw to that, but so too did his fame. Girls gave him flowers. Teams of women scrambled to row him across lakes. He touched cheeks and delighted in coquetry but there was a terrible darkness, never far away. There always was with him. Throughout this leg of his journey, the end of his marriage still weighed heavily on Lord Byron.

In his diary of the crossing, intended as a letter to his sister Augusta, he wrote:

'Arrived at Grindenwald, dined, mounted again and rode to the higher glacier. Twilight, but distinct; very fine glacier, like a frozen hurricane. Starlight, beautiful, but a devil of a path. Never mind, got safe in, a little lightning, but the whole of the day as fine in point of weather as the day on which Paradise was made. Passed whole woods of withered pines, all withered, trunks stripped and barkless, branches lifeless, done by a single winter. Their appearance reminded me of me and my family.'

It was rejection that he could not bear. Throughout his life, his love of loyalty would blind him to the foibles of the dubious characters who pledged allegiance to him. Likewise, his fear of being unloved would blind him to his own part in causing feelings towards him to change.

The need for acceptance is a strange distortion of the basic requirement for love. It equates approval, inclusion and idolatry as worthy stand-ins for receiving love, and conformity as a fine substitute for being able to give it.

It was one of the intriguingly human dichotomies of Lord Byron. On one very distinct side, he was authentically outré. On the other, he craved absolution through the acceptance of others.

Superstars just want to be loved too.

I asked to settle my bill at the Geneva B&B. The owner smiled tightly and enquired, 'Did you take a bottle of whiskey from the hall yesterday?'

'What kind of whiskey was it?' I asked. I'm not sure why. I was so affronted; it was the only response that came forth.

'I don't know. It was up here.' We were in the breakfast room. She waved at the cabinets that were, firstly, way too high for me to reach and, secondly, not in the hall. The cupboard she referred to was crammed with spirit bottles; how you'd know something was missing was interesting. Thirdly, I was out all day on the day in question, your honour.

I told her I did not steal the whiskey. I didn't even drink,

I said. She let it go because I suppose what else could she have done? It was excruciatingly awkward though, because I then had to ask her to call me a taxi and I had to wait for it to arrive. I acted all cheery and nonchalant and as if nothing had transpired, until my cab arrived, thank God, and then I got the hell out of there. It should not have mattered to me. It was so offline, so out there, one of those moments in travel that makes a great dinner party anecdote on returning home. But as my cabbie drove me from the B&B to the train station I was fuming. And as I sat on the Geneva railway platform waiting for my train to Milan, I could not shake the sense of injustice. It was there I startlingly put it together.

This was not about the B&B. This was about the fact that I used to steal as a kid. So many suppressed memories had been bubbling to the surface since I had stopped drinking. This was one of those and it had been coming up, in waves of shame and horror, quite regularly. And each time, I had chosen to shut it down. It was confronting then, to stand accused. This time, I could not do the shutdown. It had manifested externally.

I worked in a milk bar after school from age fourteen. For a while there I stole money. Every so often I paid myself double my wage. The entire extra ten or fifteen dollars went on clothing. Compulsively bought, often ill-fitting garments (it was the 1970s, everything was ill-fitting) that I would wear to the local shopping mall on Friday nights where my girlfriends Roseanne and Sandra and I hung out with boys. Roseanne and Sandra were skinny with great boobs, silky hair and brown skin and the inherent allure of pretty, well-developed fourteen-year-olds. I was developed, but chunky, short, pimpled, with wavy hair, and my teeth bore the yellowing of too much antibiotic as a small child. I make myself sound hideous. I wasn't. But this was how I saw myself.

The owner of the shop I was working in caught me slipping a tenner into my trousers. I had got bold. He was standing right next to me. He and his wife let me go not long after.

I never felt guilty while I was stealing. I felt they owed it to me. After all, the woman would pull me into the residence behind the milk bar and bitterly expound her theory that her husband was having sex with the other young girl who worked in the shop. She tried to get me to act as a spy, to report back anything I heard from him or the other girl that might confirm her suspicions. They sold the milk bar and bought another store in the inner city, to which I would travel on Friday nights and Saturdays for my shifts. After work on Fridays, the man would close the shop, turn down the lights, put a record on, and we would lie on the beanbags down the back of the shop where he would ply me with booze before giving me a lift home. Nothing seriously untoward happened. But I felt trapped into drinking with him.

In my teens I was all about being the good kid. What plagued me was not the actual stealing, but the getting caught. It was the look on the man's face as he saw me that haunted me. I gave him and his wife, both of whom I despised yet with whose strange power games I played along, an opportunity to think less of me.

Trains tend to follow rivers when they cut through mountains. The trip from Geneva to Milan afforded valley vistas of some of the world's most dramatic mountains. It was spring so I was seeing vibrant new green against the clearest of skies. There were great stony slashes where avalanches had occurred. There were voluptuously blooming orchards and old villages of the Swiss chocolate-box variety. The mountains were still snow-capped. Terraced farming cut determinedly up impossible slopes. Clouds sat puffy atop peaks, like white afros.

I was sharing the experience with a PR team preparing for the launch of a Dolce & Gabbana fragrance. We were in one of those old-fashioned carriages divided into eight-seater compartments linked by a long narrow walkway, and at Geneva, when I bustled into my little compartment with my big bags, the two young men of the team grabbed my luggage from me and hoisted it up into the racks above our seats. 'I think I broke my wrist,' the fresh-faced blond one said as he recovered from the unexpected weight. I blushed and blurted out excuses about needing to carry books. His dark, swoon-worthy South American co-worker laughed, stretched out in his seat and pulled down his sunglasses. It was early.

When the snack trolley came by and I discovered I had no euro in my wallet, their boss, one of those edgy, unfussy Italian women who can make jeans, a T-shirt and no make-up as glam as Oscar night, piped up, 'Oh, but you must have coffee! I must get it for you.' I sipped my beverage gratefully and felt like I was in Italy before I even got there. They pulled out folders and laptops and began to talk loudly and rapid-fire. 'Kate Moss—' I heard then lots of Italian I could not comprehend. 'Naomi.' 'Claudia.' It only got better as the journey went along. *Benvenuti a Milano.*

As we came out of the Simplon Tunnel on the Italian side of the Alps, I left our compartment to stand in the walkway, where the windows now looked directly onto Lake Maggiore. A sparkling sapphire in upper Lombardy's tiara of lakes, Maggiore marked my first ever glimpse of this kind of Italian geography. It was idyllic; the kind of scenery that's hard to take in, it is so picture perfect. Shuttered villas hanging over sparkling blue water. Tiny, tiered islands with boats gliding by or buzzing about. My stomach flipped with a sense of longing, and of connection. I wasn't sure if it was merely because I was now in Italy and adored it so, or if this was a place I must one day return to. The South American PR guy joined me at the window. 'I came here for a vacation with my girlfriend,' he said. 'After standing here, looking out at it, just like you, I had this feeling and I knew I had to return here.'

'I had that feeling not thirty seconds ago,' I said, wondering immediately if that was unbelievable to him. But he shrugged, nodded, extended his hands in a gesture of 'but of course'. Intuition has credence in Italy. It surprises no one.

'It's calling you,' he said. 'You must come here one day.'

His words resonated with me. I was looking for signs that I was on the right track to all I desired. This seemed to be one.

Antica Locanda dei Mercanti, my Milanese hotel, was in an old *palazzo* right in the centre of town. The airy white foyer was full of azaleas in bloom and the receptionist had the slightly detached bemusement for which Milan is famous. I was led to my room, a small, wooden-floored space dominated by a pale green and white colour scheme, with wooden ducks lining the bed head. It had a fashionable quaintness to it that made me squeal in delight. Alarmed, the eastern European porter who had shown me up to my room scurried away as quickly as she could. The room had billowy white curtains and shutters and when I threw them open onto the warm Milanese afternoon and leaned out across the window boxes, the workmen doing a renovation across the laneway all reacted as if I was Sophia Loren herself. *'Ciao bella!' 'Mamma mia!' 'Sei bellissima!'* Ah, *Italia*. My Fellini moment.

I went out walking, heading straight for Milan's famous cathedral. I'd changed from sandals into a pair of Rockports that were, I congratulated myself upon purchase back home, an excellent compromise between trainer and ballet flat. They had a Mary Jane look, but with a sport shoe sole. They were made of white nylon mesh mostly. On my way to the Duomo I walked into a shoe store in them, not a particularly posh one. The sales girl looked down at my feet with such a violent tilt of the head and shocked expression you would think I had killed two cats, split them down the middle, shoved my feet into their gizzards and sauntered into the shop so shod.

I suddenly had the desire to buy a whole new wardrobe. Sensibly, I did not act upon it.

I was in Milan briefly, mainly to go to the opera at La Scala but also, of course, because Lord Byron had passed through there. I'd seen pictures of La Scala, but they got nowhere near the real interior of that marvellous theatre. It was bordello-like with red silk walls and fringing, gold fixtures and bacchanalian masks and statues. Somehow it was also contained and elegant by way of the symmetry and order in its arched and tiered design. I sat with an Italian couple who did not speak a word of English, and I of course, no Italian. But language barriers do not perturb Italians. They chatted to me anyway, stopping with benevolently puzzled expressions as I attempted to answer them. I worked out that their son was a doctor in London, that they would love to go to Australia, and that they were massive fans of Rossini. At night's end, so was I.

Lord Byron went to La Scala. There, he met Stendhal, who was an admirer, and not yet famous. 'I was filled with timidity and tenderness,' Stendhal wrote of the night. 'Had I dared, I would have wept and kissed Lord Byron's hand ... I attempted to speak, and uttered only commonplaces that did nothing to break the silence reigning over the company that evening. Finally Lord Byron asked me—as the only one there who spoke English—what roads he should take walking back to his inn; it was at the other end of the city, near the fortress. I thought that he was wrong to try walking: at that end of Milan, at midnight, all the shops are closed; he would be wandering along solitary, poorly lit streets, and without knowing a word of the language. So out of solicitude I was foolish enough to advise him to hire a coach. Instantly, an expression of haughtiness appeared on his face; he gave to understand, with all politeness, that he had asked me for the route, and not for advice on how to travel it. He then left the box, and I understood why he had imposed such silence upon it.'

It's widely hypothesised that Lord Byron thought Stendhal's suggestion of a coach was motivated by pity for his lame foot. The city and its society had fallen for Lord Byron with all the gusto of pop fans in Tokyo. But the prism of his brokenness distorted it into despisal. They're funny things, our prisms. (It's interesting how close that word sounds to prison.)

I was at Pescheria da Claudio, a fishmonger turned local *apertivo* favourite. It is a wonderful old shop with three big steel and glass counters selling everything fishy from mussels to lobster. In the evening, it sells plates of sashimi and prawns and oysters and for the price of the meal you get a glass of bubbly prosecco. Along one wall there were benches set with knives and forks and paper placemats where well-dressed Milanese sipped and supped before taking off into the night. I carried my sashimi and glass to one of these and when I settled the man next to me raised his glass. '*Salute*,' he said. I raised my glass back and drank some of it. It went straight to my head.

As I left that restaurant, my head woozy from that half glass of prosecco, a man wandered by, leather-skinned and ruddy-faced. By the looks of him, he was living rough. He wore a shabby, dirty version of the green felt hat you'd expect to see with *lederhosen* and an embroidered white puffy shirt. He was carrying a longneck of German beer and his blue eyes were clouded over like the ocean on a drizzly, dark winter afternoon.

We were at traffic lights together. I felt sad for him. I always did now when I saw drunks who were far-gone because I had seen people at AA who had been where they were—and maybe even somewhere worse—lift into sobriety and back into workable functionality. As we waited for the lights to change, two young Italian men, clean pressed jeans and Lacoste polo shirt types with wavy luscious hair and twenty-something vigour, ran up. One positioned himself next to the man in the green felt hat and the other took a photo. The two turned to the man and elaborately explained that they were taking a picture of the non-existent scenery behind him. The man looked at them silently, his ocean fog hiding any cognisance of the disrespect. But I did not think he was entirely oblivious.

I felt terrible for him, and quite possibly for me because I identified with him as an outsider. I suspected my motivation for drinking was actually not that it was a beautiful spring night in Milan. It was one of: *Respect me, I can drink like you. I'm like you, can't you see? I am part of this. I belong.*

But I had drunk before I left Sydney. I had decided to quit the fellowship because I knew I had to see if I could stand on my own two feet, trust myself and my relationship with God to not harm myself the way I had been. In AA terms, that put me back to day one. In God's and mine, well, truthfully then, I didn't yet know. But it hadn't felt like a step backwards. There was no such thing. It hadn't been a slip. It had been a premeditated and planned test.

In AA terms, that would be a statement of 'the obsession'. In my terms it was too. About three weeks before I left Sydney for Europe, I could not shake thoughts of drinking. It began with a visit to a clairvoyant. She asked me what the health issue was that kept me from enjoying life. I said alcoholism. She said, 'You are not a drunk. If you want a little glass of something in a *piazza* somewhere you can have it.'

That was hardly a sound basis upon which to build a decision to try to drink in a controlled manner. But for the first time in a long time, I allowed myself to consider the notion that I might not be a drunk, as the clairvoyant so elegantly put it.

In the early days of my sobriety, I told some people—not a whole lot but some—about what was going on with me. And I would say a good three-quarters of those people responded by telling me they didn't believe I was an alcoholic. It bugged the hell out of me. What did they know? I was an alcoholic. I was broken. Couldn't they see? I was defective. Damaged. An unlovable mess. I wilfully gave in to self-pity, then. I wanted them to pity me too. I wanted the world to pity me. I wanted the world to see that I was not fine at all. And I wanted the world to feel bad for me and take the blame for my misery.

As the months of not drinking went by, through prayer and meditation my connection to my spirit and my God strengthened exponentially. I never fathomed the power of that till it was my only option. And then I found out how truly awesome it was. I was shown that I was perfect as is. I was shown that I was loved.

I began to feel a bit silly, being so down on myself like that. If God had big love for me and saw me as perfect, who was I to disagree and say I was broken and unlovable? I will always be grateful for my crisis because it showed me the absolutely unconditional love of God, the transformative power of it and its ready availability to anyone who calls on it. I am sure there are plenty of other, less traumatic paths to knowing God, but to experience his vigilance during my dark night of the soul was the most precious gift I had ever received. Needless to say, the self-pity fell away.

It did, however, leave me in a quandary. So I wanted to embrace life. Okay. How was I going to do that completely with this Sword of Damocles hanging over my head? There was a sense of: yes, you can enjoy life, but within limits. Though able-bodied and in full health, it felt as if I had voluntarily put a handicap on myself. What if, as I now suspected, I wasn't an alcoholic? What if I was denying myself the immense pleasure of a glass or two of wine as part of a life well lived when I could be enjoying it?

One thing I knew: I would not go back *there*. If trouble was brewing I would know what to do and I would know where to go. But if I was incapable, truly, of handling alcohol, I needed to find out. I absolutely could not live with this fear of the unknown.

I came at it from all angles—every angle except physically desiring a drink, which was bizarre to me. Mentally, I didn't seem to want one either. I knew this was why AA presented the program as an absolute. Why it instructed its practitioners to accept that they could not drink and not get all crazy with the questions. Follow the program. Submit to it. Accept that you had this thing and that you could do nothing but accept you had this thing because it would bring up obsession otherwise.

I knew all this. It still did not sway me. In fact, it gave me more fuel to follow the path I did. I prayed and meditated on it and one night it became apparent. I had divided my belief in a higher power. I believed in two: God and alcohol. Good and evil, how very Old Testament of me. I without doubt needed to unify my concept of a higher power. I needed to take away the power alcohol had over me as an unknown. If it were to grip me in addiction, then I would know what to do. If it did not, then the hoodoo would be broken.

If the right opportunity came up, I would have a glass of wine. As these things go, the day after I decided this a friend whom I trust and love rang me and said she was coming down from Brisbane and did I want to have dinner at a favourite restaurant she and I used to frequent before she moved north. I told her what I had decided. She was very cool and unstartled and supportive. And I had it, and it was nice, and it did not make me want a bottle. But it was then I knew I had some exploring to do.

That small glass of prosecco in Milan did not satiate the curiosity either. Rather, I saw the tiny tip of the tail of why I did what I did the way I did it and I knew I had to follow it till I found the heart.

6

Mira Porte

Don Jose and Donna Inez led
For some time an unhappy sort of life,
Wishing each other, not divorced, but dead;
They lived respectably as man and wife,
Their conduct was exceedingly well-bred,
And gave no outward signs of inward strife,
Until at length, the smother'd fire broke out,
And put the business past all kind of doubt.

Don Juan, Canto I

Cruise ships, out of place like Gulliver in Lilliput or Alice through the looking-glass, sit gargantuan in Venice's harbour, towering over her perfect proportions, disgorging battalions of day-trippers on greatest hits missions. They join the already burgeoning hordes that crowd Venice's tiny lanes and bridges. Touts and trinket sellers degrade her icons, clogging her once workaday markets with gaudy junk. Her gondolas, essential transport of days gone by, are now nothing more than a novelty, a ride at the funfair. Most of her shops and restaurants are given over to maximum extraction of profit from stressed and befuddled tourists. In many parts, Venice is more theme park than a city where people live, work, exist.

Yet she fairly drips with a ghostly, glamorous majesty that is distinctly her own. There is an unyielding dignity to her crumbling *palazzi* and churches, an effervescent sparkle, a beauty to her waterways, and a sigh-inducing romance to her unchanging form. The enchantment of Venice, even today, is her supernatural transcendence of all the custodians *de jour* can throw at her. But also it is the fragility of that ability to rise above it all and the fragility of the city itself. You sense that she may finally bow, crumble and sink at any moment and that you may be the last person to see her in all her magnificence.

She's a lot like love itself in that: magnificent but fragile.

In Byron's time, Venice had its own blight, not the one of mass tourism like today, but a terrible poverty, born of her assets being stripped and degraded by the Napoleonic years and by Austrian rule. She was no longer the proud republic whose influence spread throughout the Mediterranean in powerful waves. Byron loved the sense of her having fallen from grace, of being a sullied version of her once mighty self. It spoke to him of his own state. He had been an English hero. Now, he was tainted and in some instances despised.

But when he moved to Venice in 1817, it was his kind of town in more than its symbolism. It was a party town, with its yearly Carnivale and its theatres and opera halls continuing to host great works. It attracted certain literary and artistic types. There was still a rich, lively society there. Life was ripe with sensuality and glamour, defiant and orgiastic, like a party before the end of the world.

Byron too, was living life exactly like that, as if it all might end tomorrow.

'A woman is virtuous … who limits herself to her husband and one lover—those who have two, three or more are a little wild,' he wrote of Venice's female population, as he took maximum advantage of that. As soon as he arrived, he found a lover and in so doing cuckolded a husband. She did not have his attention exclusively though. His promiscuity only increased with opportunity. Opportunity, combined with his need to still the storm of regret and sadness that his mind had become, made him insatiable.

Nature, nurture and situation: how the human spirit navigates through them, in the end, is what counts. Love is the happy ending we all seek. In one way or another, we all want to express our glory and see it reflected back to us so we might truly, tangibly know it. It is the layers of impurity through which we filter that noble mission that causes variations in it, usually for the worse.

I was on a mission now to peel away my layers. This had taken me by surprise. I had set out to follow Byron as a kind of celebration of the point at which I had arrived. As a reclaiming of all I used to love. But the more I got to know him, the more I saw there was a lot about my psyche that needed to be exposed.

This nature, nurture, situation thing: I had let all three taint my quest for love. My nature: open, gregarious and sensitive. My nurture: a child of an awful parental relationship. My situation: a lifestyle that afforded indulgence and excitement with little effort, the ease of access to some of life's decadences making it a splendidly simple antidote to the terrible combination of the other two.

It was time to unravel that tangle.

'Dear Ms Julietta Jameson,

Thank you very much for your kind email and compliments for your book. It is a pleasure and honour for me and all Dal Corso family to give hospitality to you in our houses. Even if May is for us best high season it is our pleasure to offer, extraordinarily for you, the five weeks' stay at ...'

The email was from Alessandro Dal Corso, a hotelier from the town of Mira Porte, about twenty kilometres outside Venice on the mainland. When that email arrived in my inbox five weeks before I left home, I thought I'd never read the English language mangled so delightfully. It was the utter charm of it that had made me decide to stay with the Dal Corsos, even though I thought that would mean I would need to take the bus into Venice daily to get close to Lord Byron's world. But Alessandro had added:

'If my commitments allow it will be my pleasure to show you to the places of Lord Byron the Great Lover. With my personal boat for show the real Venetian Live stile. Waiting your kind reply I'm at you back and call with high regard, Alessandro Dal Corso.'

It was an offer that was impossible to resist.

And so here I was at the Villa Margherita, a sprawling pile on Via Nazionale, the main road between Venice and the university town of Padua. It was a mansion surrounded by manicured gardens and enormous trees. Statues of gods and goddesses lined the drive. An old beagle named Bella sat on the doorstep, wagging her tail at the sign of visitors.

Alessandro had organised for me to be picked up at Mestre train station and delivered to the villa. His handsome younger brother, Dario, and an effortlessly gorgeous young receptionist, Roberta, greeted me, embarrassingly lugging my hefty bags up two wide, grand flights of stairs to my room, refusing to let me carry anything other than my handbag. 'You will be comfortable here,' said Dario, which sounded like a command but one I was willing to obey.

I unpacked and settled into my room, a tiny single with a small Juliet balcony that looked out to the poplar trees edging the northern boundary of the garden. They were tall, strong and vigorous. They had a poised permanence to them, sentries that had seen them come, seen them go.

I stood on my balcony gazing out to them and remembered the two enormous poplar trees in our yard at Lavender Street. As I saw more of Europe and its trees in their natural habitat, I could only marvel at the audacity of my parents for planting what exotica they did on our average-sized Australian block. Two poplar trees that 'strangled the pipes' with their voracious search for water, my mother would complain, so clearly these were the work of my father; three willow trees, two of which destroyed sections of fence, one of which was to act like a conservatory, providing a hollow and shady outdoor space in which to enjoy afternoon beers; two pines; a passionfruit vine; a clump of bamboo that pushed another section of the fence down; a holly bush; the aforementioned lilac and snowball trees; a crab apple tree; roses, both climbing and not; hibiscus, a liquidambar and, in a token gesture to actual location, various large wattle trees, bottle brush and a couple of massive red gums. I do not assume this recollection is complete. It did not include the flowerbeds, one of which was overrun with nasturtiums, or the chilli plants that were in another garden bed for a while—again, an exotic addition from my father to a suburban Melbourne garden of the 1960s.

Years after the Jamesons left the property, 10 Lavender Street, Ringwood made the local newspaper front page when one of the pine trees crashed down, straight through the roof and into the bedroom known to us as 'the boys' room', the room that eventually became mine when the last of the boys left home.

The room was empty at the time. Still, assumed permanence proving impermanent, the latent, unconsidered danger in something I slept maybe five metres away from for years, listening to it creak in the wind at night ... I was long gone when it fell and it wasn't my drama. But I never thought that tree would come down of its own volition.

I had walked through life with an endless entourage of unacknowledged, unproven and mostly erroneous assumptions. In that moment when one of them was brought to light by finding out that its exact opposite was actually true, the rest of the myriad beliefs on an indecipherably humming background track were momentarily quietened by the possibility of being potentially wrong too. But only for a second. The mind is a self-preservation mechanism and will quickly go into lockdown at such a breach of protocol. It assumes, therefore it is. Move along, nothing more to see here.

I thought this must be what people meant when they said something gave them pause for thought. That pine tree gave me pause for thought. Even the Villa Margherita poplar trees wouldn't be there forever.

And neither would my assumptions now. I was undoing myself.

After I finished unpacking I had a coffee downstairs. The hotel was unnervingly quiet. Though Dario had assured me they were busy, mid-afternoon there was only me, Roberta and Bella the beagle amidst the lavishly stuffed sofas and expensive artworks. I wandered the hotel to the strains of Julio

Iglesias piped into every corner until I started to feel terribly claustrophobic. I had decided on the Villa Margherita because, apart from Alessandro's charming email, I could not afford to stay for weeks on end in Venice. Now I was wondering about my decision. I seemed to be so close yet so far away from where Lord Byron had lived, and trapped in what felt in that moment like a ritzy convalescent home, and there wasn't even a desk in my room and I had to write, and there weren't even any shops nearby and, and, and ... I needed a walk.

Roberta gave me directions up to the main village, which did little for my sense of isolation. 'It is about fifteen minutes,' she said in her musical Italian accent. Bella wagged her tail at me. Well at least no one seemed to be seeing the inner turmoil.

I walked out the door, crossed the busy Via Nazionale, took a turn-off to the left and found I was following a gently ambling canal with willows drooping into it and wild flowers dotting its banks. On previous travels, seeing such a perfectly tranquil scene for the first time would usually have me succumb to bliss. Not this day. I was all over the place, too panicked to appreciate the splendour in front of me. One minute my attention was grabbed by a boarded-up old villa for sale and then I was concocting an elaborate fantasy around buying it. The next I was barely breathing, constrained by the return of that feeling of claustrophobia, freaked out at the notion of staying with people I didn't know for an extended period of time. Then I forgot which direction the traffic was coming from, stepped into an intersection and almost got totalled by a speeding Mercedes. It left me shaken, wondering what I was doing here in the Italian countryside, doubting everything.

Increasingly unsettled, I rounded a corner, saw a crowd outside a shop and knew the sway of popularity suggested one of my favourite things about Italy: gelato. I am a simple creature. With a big cone in my hand piled high with scoops of banana and strawberry ice cream, all the noise and hubbub of my mind subsided.

That's when the whole outing culminated in the Lord Byron moment.

I was strolling along, placated by my gelato like a toddler with a treat, when not far up the road from the gelateria I came upon a dishevelled old villa turned into apartments, as many of the Mira villas had been. But what made this one remarkable was the sign above the doorway, barely discernible, reading, 'Lord Byron abito 1817'.

Okay. So maybe the Villa Margherita was a good choice, after all. It turned out Lord Byron had taken summer residence in Mira, along the Brenta Canal, like much of Venetian society, and here I was, a mere stroll, panic attack and ice cream away from where he'd stayed.

In the sixteenth century the Brenta River was turned into a 36-kilometre-long canal from Padua to the Adriatic Sea, bypassing the Venetian lagoon, becoming a transport channel and source of irrigation for the fertile low-lying land. Venice's noble families established estates and built villas along it, using the great architects Palladio and Preti. The houses became the summer escapes for the patricians who left their regular residences in Venice. In the summer, the Riviera del Brenta became one long revelry, with parties *en palazzi* and aboard the barges that drifted from home to home. Famous guests at the goings-on included Galileo, Napoleon, Casanova, Goethe, the playwright Goldoni, and artists Tiepolo and Canaletto.

And of course, Byron. He took up residence in the Villa Foscari, as the rundown property with the plaque was once called, and from there he wowed society with his wit and charisma, and wooed ladies with a mere blink of his liquid blue eyes.

Being so close now to the places where Byron's sexual conquests were their most prolific, I couldn't help but think about my dad. And my mum too, because if there was one person most affected by my dad's philandering, it was, of course, her. He had lovers and Mum had kids, six of them. Lord knows how many lovers he had.

But my mum was not the kind of woman you would have looked at and said, 'There goes a mother of six.' She was the flame around which moths dance. She was dramatic and sensual. She was steely strong and intensely cunning, an astounding survivor who never left us wanting for anything, really.

Though my dad was one of those men who spent his income outside the home, we had new dressing gowns when we needed them, and clean albeit well-used towels and sheets. We had food in our tummies, though often it was mince meat or a mix of egg and tomato on toast, of which we happened to be very fond. The house was cold and damp, but we had briquettes for a fire to huddle around until Mum got an oil heater on her account at Walton's. We had parties and good times and Mum had good friends. We had hugs and laughs and a warmth, as a family unit, that I understand now is rare.

But my mother had a way with a wooden spoon or a hairbrush that if we misbehaved was frightening. If you came home late for dinner, it was the most ferocious. I believed her true feelings about my dad's behaviour came out during those sessions when we would be bent over the bath, pants down, receiving our beltings. Coming home late for the meal she'd scrimped for and managed to get on the table for numerous mouths with everything else she had to do on her own due to his absence, that was a disrespect that pushed her buttons mightily.

I was ten or eleven and going through a phase of pulling sick days from school so I could stay home with her or go to the Dorset Gardens Hotel, where she worked after Dad left. She was outside, hanging some washing before we left for the pub. I don't know what possessed me. I knew she hated being called Gabby. Her name was Gabrielle. Only our father called her Gabby. For whatever reason, I stood on the back steps and yelled, 'Gaaaaaa-beeeeee!' She flew around the corner with an enormous stick in one hand, grabbed me with the other and beat me repeatedly around the legs before she crumpled at the horror of what she was doing.

Even then, I understood. I always understood with her. I knew what she had given up. I loved to look through the suitcase of old photos of her during the war. She looked happy and vigorous. She was a WAAF wireless operator and she did air force revues and plays, singing and dancing, the world before her. She was attractive and smart. And then he came along.

He was good-looking and clever, the best-looking boy in Hobart. Both my mum and dad, like Lord Byron, had dominating and perhaps unhinged mothers. In fact, Dad's mum was as controlling as Lord Byron's. She was a spectre in our lives, the tough Irish matriarch who had money that she would help us out with occasionally. She cut Dad off because of his waywardness. Her patronage of us saw us through some rough times but it was not without hooks. We were never allowed to forget we were the poor relations.

When I think about my dad and his total lack of suitability for parenting, I think of her, his mother of legendary toughness and unattractive eccentricity, and the death of his beloved sister Patty, two years older than him, when he was nine. I also think of him as a tail gunner flying missions in World War II. They didn't call the tail gun the death seat for nothing. And of him surviving a plane crash during the Korean War. No therapy, no counselling afterwards. I see his story. I feel for him. And I get him.

And then I see my mum, an only child whose mother had dementia, and whose father was a postmaster who fled Hobart and his family after embezzling to feed his gambling addiction. She never saw him again.

Her story amazed me. The resilience of the woman. Her extraordinary zest for life. But I never heard her say, 'I love you.' She did say it with hugs and kisses, scones, cakes and soup, though. That she did.

My dad died when I was in my mid-twenties, my mum in my thirties. The worst thing about the death of my parents was not being able to ask the questions that came up when I was trying to understand myself and unravel my myths. It was beyond me how or why there were six of us, their kids. The first three I got, in quick succession, spanning five years or so. But then there was a gap of six years and then another set of three kids, six years between them from start to finish. I did not get that. Not at all. Because by the time I came around, I assumed the writing was on the wall. I had also always thought that theirs was not a big love. But why would I assume that, when they were together for long enough to have that many children? That's a good twenty-five years of togetherness, more than most people achieve these days. Because of the unbridled hatred my mother would unleash about my father, and the lack of palpable attachment he had for us, I guess that was a logical conclusion.

Five years before I began following Lord Byron, I decided to write a book about my dad's life, to try to make sense of it. I did one interview for that book, with a journalist mate of Dad's. He was a good man and an honest one, an acclaimed beacon of his profession. He said he'd thought long and hard about it, and the time had come when he thought we should know: there was another sibling, a half-brother, born somewhere around the same time as Erin and me. *To the woman who was the love of our father's life.*

This was what he said. Not Dad's second wife, who had no children with him but who nursed him through cancer to his death. Not our mother, who knew him from childhood and was intimately part of his family, who moved to the mainland from Tasmania with him, set up house around him, bore him six kids. It was some other woman.

This journalist mate of my father told me the woman had been the secretary to a famous Melbourne architect. When she fell pregnant, Dad got her married off to a Polish man who needed to be married to stay in the country.

I didn't know what part of the story was more shocking. At any rate, I never pursued the book. This was clearly a can of worms I was not ready to open.

So many questions. And ones I could not and probably never would answer.

But I was also coming to know that there were questions I *could* answer. Questions about what had kept me from the love I sought. Out of my growing willingness to look at where I had come from and what made me what I was, a confidence was arising. This proximity to Lord Byron's haunts had very quickly indeed begun to give me a new perspective on my life. I was only beginning to ensconce myself in his world, but already I could feel the power in that. I was removed from my everyday.

I had given myself permission to think creatively about the sum of my experience. And I had chosen the marvellous map of Byron's world to guide me in doing that. What a great gift I had given myself.

I did not yet have the answers to any of the questions, but I could feel them coming towards me, now. I felt as if I would not need to seek them. They were preparing to find me.

7

School Days

'... I have thought
Too long and darkly, till my brain became,
In its own eddy boiling and o'erwrought,
A whirling gulf of phantasy and flame:
And thus, untaught in my youth my heart to tame,
My springs of life were poison'd. 'Tis too late!'

Childe Harold's Pilgrimage, Canto III

Life is nothing without its moral ropes and emotional padlocks. Even the great prophets and saints had them. They descend on us in our first dealings with the world at large and they do not change of their own volition, leaving the choice ours as to whether we tighten them or loosen them.

Lord Byron, I think, was too consciously fond of his. They fuelled his fire. His strange ancestry was one thing, his parents' terrifying relationship another. But to say his school days at Harrow were formative is to say Hamlet saw dead people—the mere surface of the matter. For an emotional, highly-strung imagination, they were as intense and dramatic as the lives of the Greek classical heroes in which he was educated and his whole life from there on was a series of reactions to the experiences of a very young man.

His life in Venice was so indicative of that. The partying, the sex, the utter abandonment to hedonism; he sought obliteration of those memories. In his writing, he wavered between glorifying and demonising his past. Either way, he was always, at least in part, still back there at Harrow where, as a child of precarious means and noble lineage, boarding with boys who had both breeding *and* money made him proud and determined for greatness. The bullying he received because of his lame leg would turn him into a willing pugilist, both in the school sporting ring and in more ad lib situations. Above all, the relationships he forged with other boys in an atmosphere of fags and masters, submission and adulation, would give him permission to express his most taboo desires.

It was during his Harrow days, though away from the school, that he would also fall for Mary Chaworth, a neighbour in Sherwood who was related to a poor unfortunate murdered by the Wicked Lord Byron. At eighteen, she was three years his senior when these feelings of his arose.

He would, as time went on, idealise both Mary—who in the end did not return his affections and spoke derisively of him—and Harrow, enshrining them as remnants of a golden time when the basic yearnings of his soul were neither judged nor punished, but where he learned that the romantic love of a woman was fraught.

Sometimes the paths of great men show us lessons in what not to do. Lord Byron's never-ending reacting to the slights and sublimities of his past would, in the end, contribute to killing him at the age of thirty-six.

But his passion and exuberance, his commitment to his life's expression no matter what the subject matter, the courage in his creativity, left an example to admire and aspire to, despite his negative traits. That to me meant his death was not in vain.

The backstreets behind Byron's Venetian *palazzo*, Mocenigo, were quiet save for a soprano doing vocal exercises somewhere nearby. I had been walking in Venice for practically five hours straight when I found the small lane that led to Mocenigo's back door, or as near to it as I was going to get. It was fenced off with an elaborate, expensive-looking confection of iron. I stood my side of the gate and breathed in my closeness to the place most synonymous with his legend. It was so still there. I heard the gulls and smelled the salt from the nearby Grand Canal. A man leaned out a window directly above me. '*Buongiorno*,' he said, astonishing me. He was friendly, welcoming. It was such a stark contrast to what I had thought of the Venetians: by and large, a jaded, exhausted, blasé, unwelcoming bunch.

I had discovered, though, that if you took one street away from the tried and true paths between Piazza San Marco and Santa Lucia station, you found something truer, quieter. More local. And infinitely more gracious. I looked at my map again, the infuriating map which caused me to pull out my reading glasses and take off my sunnies each time I needed to refer to it. It was so damned intricate, Venice's streets and canals and bridges so tightly entwined, they were a bamboozling puzzle, especially for someone as long-sighted as me. Yet here I was, a mere five hours into my first day in Venice (mere—yeah, right), at Lord Byron's back door. It had served me in the end.

A silver-haired *bella donna* wearing a kaleidoscopic scarf over black elegance came out the gate and didn't see me till she was on top of me. She started.

'*Mi dispiace, signora,*' I said, sincerely sorry to have frightened her. '*Io scrivo un libro a Lord Byron.*' I'm sorry, I had said. Then, I am writing a book about Lord Byron. Two of my very few phrases of Italian; two, I was discovering, very useful ones.

'Ah, Lord Byron. I am sorry but I am on my way out so I cannot invite you in,' she replied in perfect though accented English and with a warm smile. Was she the current owner? The gate seemed to fence off a number of *palazzi*. If only she had been coming home rather than going out, I thought. Again I was not expecting such openness at all. But I did want to see his view of the Grand Canal. Oh well. I looked at the confounded map again. There was another minuscule laneway just a short distance from where I was, and it came out at the Grand Canal. It looked to open onto that famously fabulous body of water only about three doors down from where Lord Byron would have come and gone on his gondola.

I doubled back from his back door, did a U-turn to my right and walked down this lane with barely any shoulder clearance, pigeons flapping indignantly as I disturbed the cool, dark dankness. And then I came out on a small pier, affording me an uninterrupted Grand Canal view. His view. Except for the San Tomà *vaporetto* stop directly across the way, where a hive of tourists bustled like worker bees to get on the crowded boats running up and down the canal, it might have been almost identical to how it was in his time. To the left was the great sweeping bend in the canal known as the Volta, and the Byzantine-Gothic *palazzo* Foscari, dating back to the sixteenth century, now decorated with a banner for abstract artist Bruce Nauman's entry into the upcoming Biennale. Across the way were egg-yolk yellow and apricot manses, their green shutters bolted against the glaring heat of the afternoon. Another large *palazzo* like Mocenigo faced off directly across the way, its crimson and gold curtains billowing out the window,' waving at passers-by.

I sat on the pier and let nothing come between his view and me. I felt his presence there. A school of tiny fish gathered at my feet. I watched them weave among the seaweed. I didn't notice the approach of a man, who now was mooring his boat next to me, as if he was parking his car, which he essentially was.

'*Scusi, signor, parla inglese*?' I asked him.

'Of course.'

'*Grazie*. Is it okay that I am here?'

'Is it okay for you?' He twinkled in that playful Italian way.

'Very much so,' I laughed. He was the sandy, blue-eyed northern Italian, craggy and brown from the sun, in the uniform of pastel polo shirt, designer jeans and loafers. And wedding ring. Yep, the flirtatious Italian uniform, all right.

'Then it is okay for me. You like the view?'

'I do.' I paused and watched him tie ropes and shuffle bits and bobs into lockable compartments on his little runabout. 'I am here because of Lord Byron,' I continued, though he didn't seem to be questioning why I was there at all.

'Oh yes? A lot of ladies have been here because of Lord Byron.'

I laughed. 'I guess so.'

'Well, he did have a good taste for ladies, I believe.' He stepped off his boat and onto the pier. 'He would be happy such a beautiful lady as you is here for him. *Ciao, signora*.' And off he went down the laneway.

I'm one to look for signs. I took this as one. It, and the nice lady at the back gate of Mocenigo: signs that I was on a good path, one of which Lord Byron himself might approve.

Later, on my way back down to the bus station from

San Marco on the *vaporetto,* I passed the front of the Palazzo Mocenigo. I waved. At who? At what? Well ... I just felt compelled to. I could still feel Lord Byron's presence there. And I thought I should go with that.

Alessandro Dal Corso invited me to the family's other property, the Villa Franceschi, for dinner. It was not far up the road, I could have walked, but Alessandro came and picked me up in his large luxury SUV. He was wearing an apron. 'My brother and I, we work in both properties, doing what has to be done,' he said. The Dal Corso boys had taken over the two hotels from their parents, but unlike so many second generations of successful business people, they weren't squandering their inheritance. Rather they were working as hard as, if not harder than, those who had built the business.

At the Villa Franceschi, twice as glamorous as the Villa Margherita and infinitely busier, Alessandro ushered me into the restaurant where Dario was also aproned and waiting tables.

'Where would you like to sit?' asked Alessandro.

'Oh, maybe outside?' I said. There was a big, inviting terrace overlooking the lawn, the nearby church clock tower and a pink and yellow sunset.

Alessandro set me up at a table in the corner of the patio. I was the only one out there. Strange, because the restaurant was full and the evening divine. Why didn't anyone else ask to sit outside? He poured me a glass of prosecco and I let it sit in front of me for a while.

It soon became apparent that the reason I was the only one out there was because the al fresco area was booked for a function. There was a surprising and quick gush of company and I was surrounded by a very large, extended German family, nibbling finger food and drinking cocktails. There was me, an island at a table, in a throng of family reunion: awkward. While at least some of the Germans seemed to find it highly amusing, the rest gave me unsure sideways glances, then chose to pretend I wasn't there. It could have been worse. I drank my prosecco, not out of wanting to, or even discomfort, but because Alessandro insisted. He kept buzzing by with the bottle, eager to please.

I ate quickly, then, hoping not to seem ungrateful, stopped Alessandro. He attempted to fill my glass again. '*No, grazie,*' I said, putting my hand over the glass. 'I'm just a bit tired. I think I'll go back to Villa Margherita soon.' He looked upset. 'It's okay. You don't need to drive me. I can walk,' I reassured him.

'I have an idea,' he said, his face lighting up, and raced off into the darkness. Shortly, I heard the trill of a bicycle bell. Alessandro, in his apron, came pedalling across the lawn.

'You must take my bike. Take it for your stay.'

Delighted, and figuring he used his car usually and not his bike, I gratefully accepted. I jumped on it, and pedalled home down the Brenta, laughing to myself at the absurdity of my evening.

The next day, I caught a glimpse of Alessandro arriving for work at the Villa Margherita. He was on a decidedly female-looking bike, with a baby seat on the back. Oh no! I'd taken his and now he was using what I assumed was his wife's. I was mortified. My instinct was to rush downstairs and insist he take his bicycle back. But what I knew of Italian hospitality was that you couldn't say no to it. To do so would be more offensive than any inconvenience they might have caused themselves by their generosity. Still, *mamma mia*. Bicycles were lifeblood transportation in the area. It was flat, the roads away from the main highway quiet. While Germans and French people in

Lycra came to cycle seriously here, the Venetians were practical cyclists; they got about their business on bikes. They cycled out for coffee, to pick up the children—some bikes had not one, but two kiddy seats; one at the front, another at the back—they cycled to the fishmonger, who set up a stall by the canal in the mornings, they cycled to the bar at night. And now someone, somewhere in the Dal Corso family, did not have a bike on which to do all that.

But I made use of that bicycle. I took bread rolls from breakfast and pedalled till I found the ducks in the canal, the little new spring chicks and their busy, protective parents. And I just rode. Between the dilapidated villas all boarded up and their neatly maintained neighbours. Past clumps of red poppies swaying gently in the breeze along the canal's banks, through fields of fruit and vegetables, past grottos with shrines to the Madonna, past ancient walls creaking under the weight of fat, pungent roses. Through thickets of pine trees and tall grasses rustling with rodents. Past Palladian architecture and farmhouses, schools, churches, locks, bridges, *trattorie* and corner stores. I rode and I sang and I thought. Sometimes I stopped and took pictures or read, or wrote, or lunched, or had coffee.

Soon, as I rode along the Brenta Canal, I noticed I was attracting incensed stares from some people. I wondered if any of them knew I had caused one of their own to be without a bike. But I think it more likely they were in some manner taken aback by an entirely foreign-looking woman riding along on a local-looking bicycle, unintimidated by trucks, stares, car doors and buses. Or maybe it was the singing. Either way, I don't think they were really irate. I think they were somewhat affronted. I was foreign acting local. But I had ridden a bike in Sydney, a place where cyclists are actively hunted, and therefore had seen it all. Secondly, and very newly, I quite liked standing out. Not belonging. Not so long ago it would have frightened me. But then, this being noticed didn't involve any interaction with people.

Interaction ... now that still scared me. No one who knew me then would have believed this, but every time a new friendship had threatened to form in my life to that point I had been terrified. I was so far behind the eight ball when it came to such things.

I didn't go to kindergarten. Everyone else in my prep grade did, and together. And while that meant I had an extra year at home watching *Ben Casey* with my mum, it put me on the outside. Everyone had best girlfriends already when I came along. In prep class, I first tried to befriend two girls who had already notched up two years of friendship. At five, this was over thirty per cent of our life span. It didn't work out, just couldn't work out, for me getting the best girlfriend I so wanted.

So next, I got a best boyfriend called Curt. He was new to the neighbourhood and had a crew cut and olive skin and he was sweet. At his house there were beehives and a rose garden in which we loved to play. Until one day, a friend of one of my older brothers made fun of our friendship, teasing me that I had a boyfriend. It wasn't the same after that. I became aware that it wasn't a regular friendship. So I tried to make regular friends.

I had discovered there was no such thing as Santa—the usual way, seeing parents put presents under the tree. My family wasn't particularly big on those kinds of myths anyway. I was still in prep when I picked out a girl called Lisa who I thought would be a good friend. As we hung our bags and cardigans on the hooks outside our classroom for the day ahead I decided to cement our friendship by letting her in on the secret, that there was no Santa. I truly believed that she would be delighted to be in the know, and that I was doing her a huge favour, giving her this present of knowledge.

She was quite upset, not the response I was expecting at all. I stood confused as she ran into the classroom, crying, to tell the teacher what I had said. The teacher came flying towards me, Lisa in one hand, and with the other, slapped me hard across the back and told me I was a wicked child. Of course there was such a thing as Santa.

Then I befriended the little deaf boy named Anthony. He already made a beeline for me every time the boys had to pick a partner to hold hands with on the walk to the toilet block anyway, so I figured it was friendship readymade. One rainy lunch hour we were being supervised in our room by a couple of grade six girls. Someone got up to sing in front of the class. Like I'd seen the boys do, I encouraged Anthony into giggling about it with me. Not out of any naughtiness. I just thought it was what boys did with their friends, so this would forever cement Anthony and me in mateship. We got caught. The grade six monitors made us get up and sing while instructing the rest of the class to laugh their heartiest at us.

Then the rain must have stopped, because everyone left the room, except for the monitors, Anthony and me. They pushed at us and pulled us and slapped us and called us things. I pleaded with them that I was wearing my best jumper and could they stop pulling it like that. They didn't for quite a while.

We've all got our stories of being bullied or overlooked or missing out on friendship. From the time I started school, my story had been one of recurring botched attempts at intimacy, where everything always went somehow terribly wrong and I was haplessly to blame.

Did this stuff bounce off other kids? Or did we all intern-alise these messages and lose track of them on the super highway of subconscious chatter, until we took the time and found the courage to tease them up and look at them? I was compiling evidence from very early on that, unfettered and unregulated, I was too much. I wrecked things when I was me. I blew things. I laughed too loud, argued too much, felt too strongly.

When Mum and Dad decided to divorce in 1972, Erin and I became the only kids in the entire school, maybe even the entire neighbourhood, to have separated parents. It was weird to be that. Nothing like Lord Byron being a peer of the realm but poor, and yet it was. We were poor and kids of divorce and yet there was a kind of allure to that. We had parties at our house and kids came and hung out. There was a sense of freedom there at Lavender Street, with Mum out working—very rare then too— and Dad not there. The Jamesons were different. Notoriously cool, my brothers were popular, handsome, charismatic boys known around the neighbourhood, good with the ladies, into music and art, generally, in many ways, their father's sons. But also their mother's sons. They had a sense of loyalty, of humour, of delight in others that they got from her. People responded to them. I basked in their reflected glory. But for me, nothing could get around the fact that we were in a middle-class neighbourhood and we were struggling. I felt dirty, damaged and broken. So unlike the other kids, who had dads at home and less freedom, less cool, but more security, more comforts. I would have given anything to be one of them.

Something was happening to me along the Brenta. I had begun to acknowledge all these things about me, and unflinchingly look at them. And unlike Lord Byron, I was thinking about letting go of them. I had not known it could be so simple. That by acknowledging things, exploring stories but not submerging in them again, or attaching to them, you could move through them and forward. It seemed like my time to get that. And intangibly, it seemed like I had much to gain from doing so. I was beginning to like that woman sitting at her lone dinner table amid the German cocktail party. She was beginning to frighten me less and impress me more. Damaged, dirty and broken was starting to look like unique, experienced and humanly flawed. That was how I considered Lord Byron. And I was starting to pay myself the same honour.

8

Padua

The world is full of orphans: firstly, those
Who are so in the strict sense of the phrase;
But many a lonely tree the loftier grows
Than others crowded in the Forest's maze—
The next are such as are not doomed to lose
Their tender parents, in their budding days,
But merely, their parental tenderness,
Which leaves them orphans of the heart no less.

Don Juan, Canto XVII

Marianna Segati was Lord Byron's first long-term lover in Venice. She managed to maintain his attention for nearly a year and a half. The wife of his first Venetian landlord, she was sexually voracious, dramatic and physically his type, with her thin body and dark eyes. There was also a tremendous sense of danger in being with her under the roof of her husband—Lord Byron and the Segatis shared the same lodging in the Frezzeria area of San Marco, an upstairs–downstairs arrangement of sensual opportunity. Dangerous, yes, but the husband in question, Pietro Segati, knew what was going on, treating it as out of sight, out of mind—such was the Venetian way of the time.

After having been in the Veneto a year, Byron decided to do some sightseeing in the rest of Italy. Marianna begged to come with him. He resisted, writing to his best friend, John Cam Hobhouse, of her as 'carnal baggage' that he was loath to carry. He was never faithful to her anyway. And needless to say, he did not take her along.

It's such an unattractive aspect to Lord Byron, the way he could so suddenly turn on the females in his life, showing callous disrespect. These are the moments in which I am torn about him. There's that big, luminous soul on display through his work. Then there is the hemmed-in heart, constricted and contorted—and reactive.

By the end of his school days he had grown to despise his over-bearing, accusative and argumentative mother, who blamed his father's side of the family for all the failings she saw in her only child. He wrote to his half-sister Augusta, 'I have never been so scurrilously and violently abused by any person, as by that woman.'

It's so tempting to try to side with Catherine Byron, a single mother in the late 1700s, early 1800s, attempting to bring up a wilful, highly intelligent son. But from her there was a dependence on him for companionship, a wild oscillation between permissiveness and berating, and worst of all, a siding with his abuser. After it came to light that ten-year-old Lord Byron's nanny, May Gray, had sexually interfered with her charge, had beaten him and most probably had sex with strangers in front of him, Catherine Byron did not dismiss her immediately. She had close ties with May's family, who insisted that reports of this wrongdoing were fabrications of a spiteful little boy. Catherine did nothing to dispel that.

Later, in the last years of his life, Lord Byron would reflect, 'My passions were developed very early, so early, very few would believe me, if I were to state the period and the faces which accompanied it. Perhaps this is one of the reasons which caused the anticipated melancholy of my thoughts, having anticipated life.'

What a life to anticipate.

Our early experiences do set up expectations, though, for all of us. Lord Byron was not alone in that. And we spend the rest of our lives playing them out. But if we're lucky, we reach a point where they no longer serve us, and if we have the courage, we can dismantle them.

Nina was a bespoke travel director who lived not far from Verona. She was an Australian of Sicilian parentage who had lived in Italy for over twenty years. Alessandro had put me in touch with her and I was to become more and more grateful for that. We spoke for the first time when she rang me in my room at the Villa Margherita. I liked her velvety voice. She had an accent that was difficult to pin down in that international way.

'Have you been to the Amalfi Coast?' asked Nina.

'No, I'm not going there till I can go with a partner. It's too romantic, too coupley. But,' I added, 'I said that about Venice too and here I am, again.'

'Have you ever been married?'

Funny, but I could never say, no, I had never been married— especially to people who were. 'I was living with somebody for seven years or so, then in another big relationship for a few years,' I hedged.

Maybe I needed to try just saying it: 'No, I have never been married.' If I was to be true to the mission of embracing the what-is-ness of me, rather than the what-isn't-ness, then I did need to find some way to be comfortable with that.

'What is the dating scene like in Australia?' Nina asked.

'Terrible,' I said, defaulting then to the 'all the single men in Australia are gay' position.

'I would have thought that in your profession there would have been plenty of opportunities.'

'I guess I might be what our grandmothers would have called picky.' That wasn't true but I said it anyway. The truth was, I didn't want to say that no one had picked me. Even thinking it felt like a betrayal of the sisterhood.

Most nights I had dinner at a rustic little trattoria up the road from the Villa Margherita. I was feeling more and more inclined to have some wine with my meal. And every time the inclination came up, I felt frightened.

Part of the AA program was about getting clear on your drinking 'story' and I never could, or rather, I didn't feel it held a lot for me. This was one of the reasons I had, in the end, left the fellowship. My story began when I had my first big drink on the night of my thirteenth birthday. It ended with me rolling paralytic into a bonfire, but I was fortunately saved from injury by my sister's boyfriend Toddy. It was awful and dangerous, but not the beginning of something big in itself. The whole narrative was something that didn't mean anything to me. Booze was always in our house and I came from a big Anglo-Irish Catholic family that drank to celebrate/console/kick back. This also did not give me the ah-ha moment. Journalists were booze hounds. I lived in nightclubs from the mid-1980s to the mid-1990s drinking vodka. I was in an intense relationship for seven years and I relied heavily on alcohol to lubricate it. But none of that felt like it had anything to do with it. It all sounded trite to me and I never felt authentic talking about any of that in AA meetings. It didn't reach the heart of the malady. I thought all those things just made it easier for alcohol to be a ready source of release from pain, whatever the hell it was caused by, and then the alcohol became a problem all of its own because it was habit-forming. It was the subtext, the back-story, that I had yet to connect with and uncover.

The true malady was a dislike of myself. Nope. That wasn't it. A disconnection from myself. Blah, blah, blah. The denial of God in my life. Not it either. I still didn't know. That was clear. But I knew I needed to find out why I did what I did. Until I knew, alcohol would still terrify me. Or rather, I would terrify myself. I couldn't trust myself until I knew why I did what I did the way I did it.

I had to move from the Villa Margherita two nights earlier than planned. I was also not sure they really wanted me to come back after my week in Rome was up as had been our original arrangement before I left home. Under that arrangement, I would come to the Veneto for two weeks, go to Rome for one, come back for another three, because Lord Byron went tripping off south from Venice to return there again and I was emulating that, albeit in a truncated fashion. Alessandro had originally offered to put me up for the whole time, but things had changed. It was fair enough that the Villa Margherita didn't want me back. They had a big booking suddenly come in and they needed that little single room I was in or else they would lose the entire group. So I'd been asked, in the nicest possible way, would I mind?

It was fair enough, yes, but it brought up sharp feelings of rejection. I said all sorts of prayers to as many guides, angels and saints as I could call in to get over it. And then I had wine with dinner. I took a sip and something in me said, 'Hello, old friend.' I was not sure it was a good idea. Nor was I sure who or what was saying that hello. I thought it might have been my head being dramatic. It had a tendency to do that. So I was not sure it was a bad idea either.

For the two nights I needed to fill between Mira and Rome, I did not choose to go and stay in Venice proper. I chose Padua. I adored that little city not even fifteen kilometres west of where I was and I didn't think I was ready for Venice yet. I believed that Lord Byron, were he a contemporary figure, would not have loved Venice as much as he did. But he might have loved Padua, a lively, intellectual and still truly Italian town. And, as if to confirm my decision, I got a good last minute deal on the internet for a brilliant little inn called the Hotel Belludi 37.

Padua is the loveliest of cities. Long colonnades and even longer porticos give it a protective, genteel sense. It wraps around you. Its interconnected *piazze* and leafy river vistas, its elegant gardens and graceful monuments have a dreamlike beauty, brought down to earth rather exuberantly by the throng of students pedalling her streets and enjoying long *apertivo* times on her sidewalks.

Part of cobbled Via San Francesco is a sweet little arch of a Roman bridge, below which is an outdoor restaurant on a small island, water trickling over pebbles, dense foliage and towering trees either side—the kind of place that would be sheer perfection for a date. As I walked across the bridge very much on my own, gazing at this romantic little spot, I became aware of a man nearby playing piano accordion. It was the melody I always heard as '*Oh, Solo Mio*'. I knew that tune was a piano accordion standard. But still. I mean, really.

'Does he have to rub it in?' I said out loud to myself,

startling the young couple next to me who had paused to take pictures of each other on the bridge. '*Solo? Mio?*' I gesticulated exaggeratedly to explain to them my situation, and followed with an apologetic laugh before continuing, 'Me, alone ... I was thinking how nice that restaurant down there would be for a date and ...'

'It's okay! He's singing "*O Sole Mio*",' the young lady said in an American accent. 'It actually means "my sun". It's a happy song. Be happy!'

Life really was all about perception.

Somewhat embarrassed, I thanked her for the clarification—I should have at least bought myself an Italian phrase book by now—and kept walking till I saw the exotic spectacle of the upper reaches of the cathedral of sant'Antonio di Padova rise above the regulation red rooftops and shuttered three-storey flat façades that characterise Padua. The church is Byzantine-inspired perfection with its blue domes and towers and a brilliant gold angel at the top.

Saint Anthony is the patron saint of lost things. 'Pray to Saint Anthony' had been a fallback position in my family for as long as I could remember, for anything from lost keys to lost loves, with mixed results. I decided to visit him and put in a prayer for my romantic heart. I thought maybe I'd lost it, or at least the essence of it, along the way somewhere. I was a great lover of Saint Francis of Assisi and so was Saint Anthony. They were both exponents of keeping things simple, unlike Lord Byron. And unlike me. Perhaps it was time for me to start following their example.

It could get crowded inside the church, but it was a Monday when I visited so there was hardly anyone there. Most monuments are closed on Mondays in Italy, so day-trippers stay away, making it a great time to see the ones that aren't closed. I marched straight up to Saint Anthony's side. It was odd to be so suddenly and easily next to the bloke whose schtick had been a family punch line my entire life. It turned out that in Padua Saint Anthony was also known as the Saint of Miracles. He'd pulled off innumerable miracles of all kinds across the years. This has turned him into one very popular saint. Either side of his sarcophagus there were boards full of photos and letters, thanking him for various miracles performed. My eyes fell on one picture, a standout for me amidst the snaps of babies, and of young, now thriving men pinned to the photos of the horrifically wrecked cars they survived thanks to the workings of the saint—or so their families evidently believed. The photo that caught my eye was of the wedding of two people in their forties looking very happy indeed. It was a casual, modern wedding; she in a simple dress, he in light pants and open shirt. They were healthy and handsome. Maybe I subconsciously went looking for it. Whatever the machinations, it was that photo which got my attention over all those other assorted miracles.

And then I sat down next to Saint Anthony to say a prayer of my own, so succinct it surprised me. No mucking around, it came out without much thought, clear and concise.

Dear Saint Anthony, I state here and now that I do want a husband or husband equivalent, a partner-type person. A loving partner whom I adore and who adores me and who will love, support and inspire me and I him. And who will be my companion on the journey of life from here on in. Who will respect and nurture me, care for me and I the same for him. May we be passionate about each other but not possessive, jealous or argumentative. May we weather storms, bask in sunlight and be lovingly, happily committed to each other for the rest of our lives. May we have fun and may we make each other laugh. And may we fancy each other like mad.

I did want that person in my life. I absolutely did.

I left the church, turned a corner and was confronted by some graffiti which read, 'Nice shoes, wanna fuck?' Now, I am one to look for signs. I did then hope that this was not Saint Anthony's message back to me, perhaps saying that my prayer was a stretch and the best I could hope for was superficial sex based on choice of footwear and such.

I found it hilarious: a haiku encapsulation of Italy's shoe fetish, which I had noticed was more than a hypothetical stereotype. It was just ironic that the poignant graffiti should be in Padua, a city of students for whom Converse sneakers were *the* shoe. They were in the minority in these parts though. As I had noticed elsewhere in the north of Italy, here continued an insistence on fabulous footwear. Of particular head-turning value were ballet flats that combined chic with practicality.

I sat down to an *insalata di tonno*, or tuna salad, on a fresh white tablecloth beneath a cool awning opposite the blushed bricks and Byzantine grace of La Basilica di sant'Antonio. Children who looked like children chased pigeons in the square in front of the church. The boys hadn't been Beckhamed to fashionable absurdity. The little girls were in simple bright sun frocks, no tweeniness about them. Italian children still had an innocence to them that was sometimes missing in other places.

A woman 'of a certain age' (as someone no doubt had noted of me) sat down at the same café in which I lunched. She had a *panino* and a glass of wine and the way she was dressed suggested to me that she was trying a bit too hard. It was all a bit Diane Lane in *Under the Tuscan Sun*. Why did she bother me so acutely? Probably the mirror. It reminded me of that unproductive state in which I had spent tracts of my life. If I do this, if I go here, if I wear that, if I cross my legs in this manner, if I create a world in my head and in my physical appearance in which I am not so, so lonely, then I can keep from falling down that black hole of utter, utter despair.

Was I that person still? I didn't think so. The evidence was not in what I did, where I went, what I wore or what I said. It was in the fact that I was no longer afraid of black holes. When they rose up along the pathway, rather than being afraid to fall down them, I knew to hold God's hand and go down them. Going down those holes, holding God's hand and knowing there was light at the other end, that was to go towards clarity itself.

After lunch I took a seat in the Padua botanic gardens, supposedly the oldest in the world. They display the same dichotomy as so many old Italian gardens: order around classical sculptures, meandering gravel paths and mathematically perfect garden beds, all juxtaposed against a created woodland. It was sunny and warm and a nice place to ponder. I heard a thrum from the woodland treetops, like the purring of a cat in small bursts. A short, vital woman of about sixty, dressed in a contemporary no-nonsense style that nonetheless showed personality and flair, followed the noise with binoculars.

'*Parla inglese?*' I asked.

'*Si,*' she said.

'What is that bird?'

'It's a woodpecker,' she replied in a well-to-do English accent. We chatted about the types of woodpecker in England and the fact that we didn't have them in Australia.

'Did you know,' she said, 'that they have unique skulls

which prevent them from getting brain damage? When they first designed bike helmets, they studied woodpeckers' heads.'

I did not know. No, I did not.

'They don't do bird watching in Italy, you know,' she said, amused at herself. 'They see the binoculars and they find it very funny. There's not even a term for bird watching in Italian.'

Yet here she was, in Italy, by herself, embracing her passion.

The palpable difference between the woman in the café and the birdwatcher was immense. I hoped I was moving closer to the birdwatcher's mien.

Mornings in Padua are idyllic. There is a buzz at Piazza delle Erbe, overlooked by the magnificently colonnaded medieval Palazzo della Ragione with its arcades of providores underneath selling cheeses and meats and crusty breads. Red cherries and strawberries and fresh white asparagus and those wonderful corrugated tomatoes from Sicily were on sale at the stalls in the square. At the cafés surrounding Piazza dei Frutti to the back of the *palazzo*, rosy-cheeked *bambini* ate little snacks of gelato from cups while their mammas rested a while with a coffee after the market.

Padua is also home to an ancient university where Galileo taught, hence all the students. Part of it comprises the Conservatorio Statale di Musica 'Cesare Pollini', where some outrageously talented person was playing piano when I wandered by later that day. It made it impossible for me to walk any further and, as luck would have it, there was a café right there, so I sat down.

I didn't know what they were playing. It had that swirling emotional landscape of Shostakovich. Everyone else at the café was chatting. The man inside had his radio on. I guessed he heard it every day. But I was in raptures.

An elderly lady, thin, fine boned, her straight, thick, once-black, now steely hair cut into a long fringe at the front and hanging down her back in a pony tail, smiled at me as she approached on foot, the crags of her face drawing into a map of the joy she had obviously collected in her life.

'You are enjoying,' she said and nodded her approval.

'*Si*,' I said, '*bellissima*.' Why I insisted on speaking a snippet of Italian to Italians, I don't know, because all it did was create an awkward moment. She began showering me with lilting phrases of pure Italian. And I had to apologise for the deception. I did not speak her language, *mi dispiace*.

'Ah,' she said, and laughed melodically, before sitting down at my table. 'So, what are you doing here in Padova?'

I told her I'd just come from the Scrovegni Chapel, where one of the most important pieces of art in the world, Giotto's astonishing Biblical cycle—widely recognised as kicking off the three-dimensionality of Renaissance art—adorns the walls and roof. It is a series of intricate frames, each fresco depicting a story from the New Testament.

'I was so moved by the picture of Jesus washing the Apostles' feet,' I said. 'But not the main part of the image. I liked how Giotto captured this sense of deep humility in the old Apostle undoing his sandal off to the side, getting ready to accept the gesture himself.'

'I like that too,' she said, in a congratulatory tone.

'The look on his face is completely stripped of guile but full of the magnitude of the moment,' I said.

'Accepting the gifts from God, this is what this picture is a message of.'

'Ha, absolutely,' I said. 'We have such resistance to

accepting gifts from God, don't we? Believing that they are gifts and not things that we've hard-earned through manipulation, anticipation, bullet-dodging, compromising and settling.'

'Oh, *signora*.' She shook her head at me. 'In Italy, our *bambini* are taught that they themselves are God's gifts to us and so, like Christmas, there will be an exchange. Gifts will be given to them. From us, from God.'

'I had to work hard for affection, for any kind of attention,' I said, surprising myself. It is amazing what comes out of your mouth to complete strangers when travelling. 'Or at least, I felt I had. Don't misunderstand me. My mother was a great woman. But when you are the youngest of a large family with much drama going on around you, and your mother, working her hardest to keep things afloat by herself, relies on your older siblings to help raise the babies, well, you know, all the adult rationale in the world is not going to fix the fact that babies see the world two ways. Either connected to Mum, or not. We are strange creatures, human beings. So susceptible. I guess I did not, never felt, I was a gift.'

'Are you married?'

God, that question. 'No.' There. I said it.

'Has a man ever treated you as his gift?'

I felt winded. 'I honestly do not think so.'

'So you thought they were the gift, and you the receiver of small mercies. My dear, you must think of yourself as this gift. You must think of Jesus washing your feet. Whenever you have thoughts of not being this gift, think of that picture.'

You know those moments when the show reel of an aspect of your life starts to run? The projector suddenly whirrs like someone's kicked it into action? This was one of those.

My mother probably did not pick me up a lot. Not out of negligence, she didn't have much time to. That didn't make her a bad woman. It made her someone who had six people—seven, including herself—to keep sheltered, clothed and fed. Acknowledging that as a probability, I saw the strange conga line of men, all unavailable in one way or another, that I'd attracted; saw them so clearly. And myself so clearly. I had this intensity, this clinginess, this terrible fear of loss, and a burning need for physical closeness with a lot of them. One of these men, a jazz musician who, when all is said and done, was always honest with me, actually once said, 'You poor affection-starved girl' during one of these episodes of clinginess. He didn't say it to put me down; in fact, he said it sympathetically. But it was a succinctness that was way too much for me at the time. It frightened and belittled me. Bless him. He was bang on the money. I wish I'd had the maturity or insight then to consider that. Instead, I retreated from his friendship embarrassed, and moved on to some more unconscious, unattainable object of adoration.

Now, not much less than twenty years later, here was this elegant Italian lady and the painting of Giotto illuminating the lesson for me. Maybe Saint Anthony heard that prayer of mine, after all. Maybe that *bella donna* in a sidewalk café in Padua was another step in my miracle of the heart.

9

Rome

Oh Rome! My country! City of the soul!
The orphans of the heart must turn to thee ...

Childe Harold's Pilgrimage, Canto IV

Rome made a tourist of even Lord Byron, the man who had his issues with tourists. He hilariously but cruelly described English vacationers as 'a parcel of staring boobies, who go about gaping and wishing to be at once cheap and magnificent'. And there he was, staying amongst them, in the English tourist enclave of Piazza di Spagna.

Lord Byron rode his horse across Rome's vast length and breadth, only dismounting for 'poring over churches and antiquities'. As he explored, he acutely sensed the layers in the city, seen and unseen, tangible and intangible. Those outings inspired much of the lauded fourth canto of *Childe Harold*. And it caused him to get personal about place. Though only in the Italian capital for three weeks, by the time he left he felt: 'There must be a sense or two more than we have as mortals, which I suppose the Devil has (or t'other) for where there is much to be grasped we are always at a loss and yet feel we ought to have a higher, more extended comprehension,' or so he told his publisher, John Murray.

There are few places in the world where history and its ghosts can affect an individual as much as Rome. The sheer volume of art and archeology, the layering of ages, at least to the imaginative, are irresistible provocateurs. And if you have ghosts of your own to deal with, they may well come up to meet you in Rome, if you are open to them.

I could see the Vatican from my bed, without even straining. Four fluffy white pillows, in a bed that could fit three people without touching, propped me up. The sheets were ironed and fine and I slid my legs this way and that relishing their silky smooth coolness. Through the double doors *a sinistre*—that's to the left, *grazie*—there was the dome of Saint Peter's glowing a gloomy blue, a bright amber crown at the higher, narrower circumference. I'd been in some corker hotel rooms, but this suite on the eighth floor of the InterContinental de la Ville took the title. It was costing me more per night than practically my entire budget for several *weeks* in other places, despite the company who ran the hotel giving me a couple of nights gratis because I was writing travel stories about it. And they'd given me a crazy upgrade. I went dizzy thinking about the full cost of what I was privy to. It would be worth it, though, if you could afford it. One day, I said to myself. One day ...

The space that had been assigned to me could inspire some terrific poesy—as Lord Byron called poetry—if you were so inclined. (Which I was not.) It had a view of the whole city from a large private terrace. I was on the top floor, above Piazza di Spagna, and so at one of the highest points in the city. On the other side of the building, because my suite extended that far, I could sit on the loo and look out an open double window across the Villa Borghese.

It wasn't the InterContinental's fabulousness alone, though, that was making me feel giddy with delight. Out of the blue, like a burst of sunshine through cloud, I believed in my right to be there. The last three times I had been to Rome, as much as I had loved it, I had felt like a ghost, wafting unseen from one spot to the next, trying to stick to something, make some impression, but never doing so. Timid, and unworthy, I hoped to not offend, not get in the way, not make a fuss, exactly as I had as a kid when all was chaos around me.

But on my first night in that glorious city on this trip, I was back in my splendiferous room having been out for dinner when suddenly I had the profound realisation of who I was and my own realness. My *realness*. It was the strangest feeling, like a potent painkiller wearing off. Bang! An invisible barrier dropped away and I saw that I was part of the history of the city. I felt connected. I saw that I had left my footprints on it. They might not name a café after me as they had after Lord Byron, or put up a monument to me, but I was part of this city. I could walk its streets and believe in my right to be there.

This day I began to believe in my right to my life. To my dreams coming true. To my happiness. Amazing what crisp white linen and a great view can do. But of course, there was much more afoot than that.

I had a salami and mozzarella toasted focaccia for breakfast the next morning, my first on this trip to Rome. The bread, closer to Turkish than focaccia, was as oily as the filling. That sandwich was delicious. I was in a bar on busy Via Tritone, it was only three euro and, as I was a creature of habit, I figured a week's worth of salami *panino* breakfasts wasn't going to hurt me, especially at that price.

The cashier knew everyone on the street. She would stand outside and smoke and wave with that Roman 'I don't give a shit' attitude. She talked on the phone constantly. How often could a cashier in a tiny café really need to talk on the phone? Maybe she was an SP bookie.

Later that day I took public transport out to the Appian Way, where Lord Byron went into a fit of poesy about the Tombe de Caecilia Metella. Even today, it was a rapturous sight; for me, quite unexpectedly so. I had not been moved by ancient Rome. The Pantheon totally floated my boat, the way it sat amidst mayhem, a squat bastion of cool endurance with a McDonald's opposite and a million eyes on it. But the Colosseum, which Byron liked—what boy who had seen it didn't?—had in the past totally creeped me out. Moreover, the Forum and the Aventine had left me unmoved. Cold.

Perhaps this had a lot to do with my disconnection from my own history. To look back that far had been too confronting. In the elegant, sparse, stripped-back ruins lay too much room for imagination—and for ghosts. With Renaissance art, which I adored, how I was desired to feel was guided by the lavishly detailed realisations of brilliant minds. There, however, amidst the remains of lives past, lay opportunity for projection and invocation. A canvas prepped only, ready for me.

But I was moved by Caecilia's tomb. I enjoyed the stirring ghosts. I found myself interested in the stories behind the structures, as I was truly now interested in the foundations of this construct known as me. She meant nothing to me, this Caecilia, the daughter of Quintus Metellus, the conqueror of Crete. But for the first time, I felt the personal in the history. Both my mum and dad had studied Latin and the ancient history that went with it. They both loved it, one of the few things they had in common in the end. I wished they were alive for me to ask about what I was seeing. But then, I didn't need too much more information than what the little plaques at various points throughout the ruins were giving me. I opened myself to the atmosphere and the more latent information and let it inform and move me.

The walk from the quiet area where Caecilia was entombed to the bus stop where I would catch transport back to the centre was quite something else, however. At the place on Appia Antica where Saint Peter supposedly met Jesus and decided to go back to Rome and face the music, it went from an easy amble to a dreadful feat of endurance along an increasingly narrow roadside as traffic barrelled towards me Le Mans style. At one of the most sacred sites in Christendom, the Romans drove at their aggressive best. For the unsuspecting tourist making their way to the bus stop, it was intense like few other pedestrian experiences.

Gosh, but this was a different Rome from that which I had seen before. The first two occasions I'd visited I'd spent every night drunk and therefore, I was guessing, every day hung-over, or at least at a level of stupefied, dulled, removed absence. The last time I was in Rome I was six months into sobriety and frightened. I was white-knuckle riding the evolving story, begging God to keep me safe. Bargaining with Jesus. Fortunately, the punishing God was a falsehood, as fake as I thought I was. A committee of angels guarded me then, closely. They were taking shifts, keeping vigil over a soul in its dark night. I was in accommodation out of the centre, and although the beauty of the city surrounded me, I didn't see it in all its bright colours. I was not enjoying life. I was surviving.

But now Rome had become for me the 'At last, I live' place of which Henry James wrote. This city had caused far better writers than me to gush. Lord Byron was at his most flowery, flouncy, poncy, lordly when he came to Rome.

Like them, I loved every little detail of it. Even as I arrived in Rome, sitting in my taxi from the train station I'd spied in front of us a woman riding tandem on the back of a motorbike, absolutely giving it to her boyfriend who was trying to drive, berating him in his right ear, her hands going a million gestures a minute, as Romans do. It was so passionate and dangerous and Roman—and I was mesmerised. In Sydney I probably would have gone into a fit of road rage. Here, it was enchanting.

It always takes me a couple of days to get the hang of crossing the road in Rome each time I visit, and when I do, it feels like such an accomplishment. This is in a stark contrast to how Sydney's disregard for pedestrians usually sends me into an 'I'm walking here!' episode of entitlement. In Rome, you just have to succumb to the traffic's rhythms, develop nerves of steel, but also balletic judgment. You can't just launch into the traffic with your head held high and eyes forward as I've seen some tourists do, frighteningly. Stopping times and distances need to be factored in, slight gaps in the traffic need to be taken advantage of so motorists have time to see you, but so too does your level of confidence because a Roman driver can sniff a chicken like a fox and will certainly play chicken with you if you hesitate.

On my first full day in Rome this time, that trepidation a foreigner feels before venturing into the hurly-burly of traffic delivered a moment. A handsome, well-suited man walked assuredly onto a zebra crossing on the insanely busy Via Tritone as only a Roman can do. I needed to cross the road, too, and decided to use him as a human shield, but he was a way away so I ran to catch up to his wake. He sensed me, or heard my necklaces jingle as I ran up behind him. The two of us made it across the road, and he turned to me and laughed, clearly amused. I said '*Grazie*', he said '*Prego*', and the two of us then went in separate directions.

Oh, those men. I couldn't get enough of the impossibly handsome Roman males. The catwalk-ready women, too. Such people would have caused me crazy amounts of insecurity back in Sydney. I even adored the plethora of policemen who looked as if they had been sent to the House of Hotness for their uniforms. They were way better dressed than the officers back home. On this score, I knew it wasn't just a figment of my state of mind in this fantastic city.

I loved, too, how Rome could deliver the unexpected. There's an eccentricity to the city made all the more whimsical by the grandness of the backdrop. One night, on Via del Corso, I saw a collective of rollerbladers, incongruously outside a very grand church indeed. It was some kind of informal roller derby. There were young guns mixing it up with the forty-somethings, the latter group including one guy with flashing disco light wheels. He was getting busy with the high-speed, front-to-back splits move. I don't think I ever saw that move for real in the day when rollerblading was big, only in the movies and video clips. It was totally rad.

The thing I loved the most about this Rome visit, though, was that I was, coincidently, a stone's throw away from where Lord Byron stayed. I could stand on the crowded Spanish Steps and wave an enthusiastic *ciao* to him on his balcony at number sixty-six Piazza di Spagna and no one batted an eyelid. Except perhaps Lord Byron.

*

Lord Byron's statue at the Villa Borghese sits on Viale della Pineta and he is broken. His book and foot are snapped off. He wears his beloved cloak, which he wrote about in his letters as if it were an invisibility shield. He and I had the opposite problem. I was seeking to be more visible after years of hiding. He was always lamenting the trappings of fame but, in spite of himself, continued to court infamy.

My hiding wasn't of the outward kind. No one who knew me would have called me a wallflower. It was much more about hiding the inner me, in particular the one that might not be liked. For many years, whenever I had to confront someone at work I would experience something like severe stage fright. I would get sick to the stomach, almost to the point of vomiting. My heart would palpitate dangerously, or so it felt. I would shake visibly. And when my mouth opened I would tear up. I was desperately afraid of being disliked. To stand up for myself and speak my truth was devastating.

When I drank, I could tell people the cold hard facts as I saw them with an acidic tongue, a razor-sharp wit and a holier-than-thou sense of righteousness. I drunk-dialled, drunk-emailed, drunk-argued, drunk-pontificated.

In the morning I would be like a cartoon character in my exaggeratedly clichéd reaction. I'd be lying there, slowly coming out of slumber, and my mind would drift to the night before. Pieces would at first slowly fall into place then gather pace, like dominoes, till the switch would be flipped, the memory of the outburst would land, and my eyes would snap open, wide and terrified, accompanied by a deep, loud gasp. Let the self-flagellation begin.

Drinking gave me so many excuses, reasons and opportunities to beat myself up. But then, self-abuse had become my stock in trade.

I felt unduly blessed when, at the end of my HSC year, my mother and older sister Bernadette won Lotto. It was 1980 and it was $150 000 between them. For my mother, it meant paying off her War Service Loan, selling the decrepit Lavender Street home and buying a much nicer, warm and sound house in a prettier part of town.

By this time, she had stopped working nights in the pub. She had put herself through secretarial school to brush up her skills, cleaning the school's premises with Erin's and my help to pay for her time there. And she had got herself a job as the secretary to the principal at the local primary school where she was happy. What an incredible woman she was. While doing all this, she still had Erin and me dependent at home.

After she won Lotto I had a room in that house on Pinewood Avenue and I gained the freedom to go to university. I was told by one of my siblings that I had been afforded opportunities they never had; and it was true, I had. The three oldest had to go out and work as soon as possible. There were three other little kids at home and one income, my dad's, a good portion of which did not make it home. But I went to Monash in the post-Whitlam years when university education was still essentially free. I worked through high school and I worked while at university. And the timing was not my fault.

Did I feel guilty still? It sure sounded like it. On this trip to Rome so many of the paintings that had caught my eye had been of Saint Jerome and Mary Magdalene in penitence. I'd never noticed them before; now it seemed every second one I saw was of them. I really was being prodded to pay attention to these mea culpa tides that had pulled me under time and again.

Sitting there at the base of Lord Byron's statue, I looked to my left and saw what appeared to be a lovers' lawn, there were so many young couples a mere piece of fabric or two from copulation. And for some, I was sure the fabric had ceased to be a barrier. On this heavenly spring day, everyone was in couples, and not just on the lawn. They were on tandem cycle contraptions, bathing their feet in fountains, walking hand-in-hand, lying across benches, one asleep in the other's lap. And who or what did I have? A dead poet and a notebook. I knew I was lucky and I was living a dream. But I did wonder how these cards had fallen. If I had chosen this single life, why had I? And how?

I looked at Lord Byron's love life and his choices were clear to me: strumpets, married women and older, sassy confidantes. The choices of a man for whom marriage was a disaster, whose mother was domineering and crazy, and whose particular passions probably suited him to the single life anyway. As he so exquisitely put it in the fourth canto of *Childe Harold*:

> The thorns which I have reaped are of the tree
> I planted,—they have torn me,—and I bleed.
> I should have known what fruit would spring
> from such a seed.

Somewhere along the way did I choose this single life? Or was it chosen for me? Was it why I drank the way I drank with seemingly no control over it? And so did I choose that or was it chosen for me? I looked at all the easy intimacy surrounding me and thought back to my last big relationship, with the man who I drove to the bank before I went to Aceh, the man who had not been able to use the L word, who despised me using it and who kept my contact to his timetable of availability and tolerance.

I would have one or two glasses of wine with dinner with him, and pick up a bottle on the way home—or have already bought one and have it at the ready—to fill the cavernous loneliness of it all. And I put up with this for way too long. He was a serial breaker-upper and I was a serial taker-backer. Wine definitely helped to smooth the edges of the idiocy of that. It was the companion he wasn't.

I watched those lovers some more, on the lawn at the Villa Borghese, being caressed by the warm Italian sunshine, a seductive breeze and each other, and injustice began to consume me. Then I sensed him. My dad. It felt like he came and sat down next to me under that statue of Lord Byron. It was such a strong presence. It felt like an embrace. Part of me melted into it. Then another part rose up.

'Fuck you,' I found myself saying out loud. 'You did this to me. You did this. This is not my fault. I did not choose this. You chose this. You were the worst male role model imaginable. You did this to me. I didn't do it. You did.'

I got up and turned to face where I had felt him. 'I need you to say sorry. I need to hear you say it. I need you to own this as your fault. I need to hear you say sorry.'

I cried a terrible release. Fortunately, such displays of emotion are everyday in Italy. No one reacted. Not even my dad. I couldn't feel him there any more.

As my last touristy thing in Rome before packing and dinner, I visited the Keats–Shelley House. The building, next to the Spanish Steps, was where another poet, poor young John Keats, died of tuberculosis. I'd been there before, on my first trip to Rome. I was glad I left returning till my last day. There was some cool Lord Byron paraphernalia in there. I saw his right-slanting handwriting in some correspondence on display, a mask he wore to some Carnivale or another, and a portrait of him so unlike the other dandified ones I had seen. His hair looked thin and his cheeks sunken, his expression was as if he was over it all, like he had the mother of all hangovers. It was an unusual portrait. His neck looked smooth, pale and long, a stunning feature I had not noticed before. I felt like I knew him better having seen the picture. He said about it: 'I happen to know this portrait was not a flatterer but dark and stern, eyes as black as the mood in which my mind was scorching ...'

Dark and scorching moods could change my face too.

In the final months of our relationship, right before I went to Aceh, that man who could not use the L word invited me to a picnic with his friends at a quaint harbour-side reserve. He suggested we leave the friends on the picnic blanket and go for a walk along the rocks, just the two of us. When we were out of sight of them, he took the opportunity to tell me that the holiday to Bali we were planning together was not going to happen as we had discussed for months on end. He was going to take it by himself. No explanation, that was the way it was.

He performed such rug-pulling tricks many times on me but this one was a particular shock because things were going well for once between us. He'd taken me on a picnic with his best friends! All was well with the world! We were a real couple!

We returned to that blanket and his friends with me in a markedly different mood. I was not of a mind, nor of the ability, to pretend at that point. I was in a full-blown, black sulk.

He was as happy as a lark.

Later, back at his place, I had calmed down. 'See?' he said. 'You look so beautiful now that you're happy. You looked so ugly all afternoon.'

I took this to heart. Again, being myself, expressing my truth had turned into me wrecking something, in this instance, my attractiveness.

Did I date men like this because, in the absence of my

long-dead father, I wanted to hear some other man apologise to me? And when they didn't was this why I drank? Close, but no cigar. There was more to this picture. It was multi-faceted, a lot like that picture of the poet.

I found a postcard of it in the museum's souvenir stash and bought it. In it, I saw Lord Byron's melancholy for real, his beauty, his charisma and the darker side of him. That picture deepened my regard for him.

And in it I saw that I was all of my faces, not only my happy ones. And that someone apologising to me for slights real or imagined was not going to change that. It was up to me to love and respect all those faces. If I didn't, no one else was going to.

Later that day, I lunched with a work contact, a debonair Roman man who flirted expertly with me and told me I was 'almost perfect' when, at the end of the meal, I did not put sugar in my espresso. 'But perfect, it is too hard. Almost perfect is much better,' he added.

Okay, Dad, I got the message. For today, at least.

Oh Rome, city of my soul.

10

Venice

So we'll go no more a roving
So late into the night,
Though the heart be still as loving,
And the moon be still as bright.

So We'll Go No More A Roving

'The mumming closed with a masked ball at the Fenice, where I went, as also to most of the ridottos, etc., etc.; and, though I did not dissipate much upon the whole, yet I find "the sword wearing out the scabbard", though I have but just turned the corner of twenty-nine.' So wrote Lord Byron of his exhausted state to his publisher back in England, John Murray, having just completed his odyssey through the Venice Carnivale of 1817.

Up all night and all day for the duration of the 'mumming' as he called it, using an old English word for ritualistic entertainment, he'd been a fixture at the gambling houses, the balls and the parties. There'd been dramas with ladies and their husbands, with ladies and other ladies, with men whom he had cause to 'punch in the guts', with servants and gondoliers, confidantes, cohorts and confrontations. And he pulled up with the mother of all comedowns.

Lord Byron had moved from the Frezzeria, taken

up residence in the Palazzo Mocenigo by now, and by his own admission was living in a 'Sea Sodom', extravagantly, promiscuously and growing corpulent from excess. He had pets of all kinds, monkeys, peacocks and dogs, all living indoors and terrorising visitors on the stairs. He claimed to have slept with over 200 women. Who knows how many men? His friend Percy Shelley was horrified when he laid eyes on him, Mary Shelley dismayed.

He was not unconscious of it himself. He wrote to Murray:

'If I live ten years longer, you will see, however, that it is not over with me—I don't mean in literature, for that is nothing; and it may seem odd enough to say, I do not think it my vocation. But you will see that I shall do something or other—the times and fortune permitting—that, "like the cosmogony, or creation of the world, will puzzle the philosophers of all ages". But I doubt whether my constitution will hold out. I have, at intervals, exorcised it most devilishly.'

The statement was a poignant harbinger of what was to come.

Excess is never for its own sake. It is a symptom, not a cause. It fills us up to push things down. The problem is, you have to keep topping up. Otherwise all that stuff that's been pushed down, buried and obliterated is going to come bubbling to the surface. Better out than in, though, because if we keep pushing it down it's eventually going to, at best, eat its own way out, at worst, consume us.

I had felt such resistance to coming to stay in Venice. I couldn't make my five-star expectations meet the reality of my budget. The greater proportion of Venetian accommodation is overpriced and underwhelming, unless you have the dollars to do it well. My timing was terrible, too. It was the lead-up to Biennale, Venice's two-yearly arts extravaganza, and the city was full.

But the resistance was deeper than that. It was the romance thing, no question. Being solo in a city of honeymooners was not enjoyable. As much as I ended up loving the Villa Margherita down the road, each morning I had been the only single person at breakfast, let alone the only solo woman. Every other table had been taken up with couples. Not even groups. All couples.

At least I'd managed to find myself a modest apartment in Venice, which meant no confronting breakfast situations. And a place to retreat to without running a gauntlet of having to say two good mornings or afternoons to people joined at the hip.

It was no Palazzo Mocenigo but, though small and basic, it suited my purposes and had some charm. Essentially it was two rooms: a kitchen with a table to eat and work at and a bedroom with a couple of little beds and an old oak chaise. There were glazed terracotta plates on the walls and exposed wood beams and tiles on the ceiling. I had a tiny bathroom, too. I could see the water if I stuck my head out the bedroom window. I was on the third floor of an old, skinny, typically Venetian apartment block accessible by a killer steep stairway with low head clearance and very little width. The block was on a narrow laneway, a dogleg between the Cannaregio Canal and a small *campo* where a deconsecrated church was busily being decked out for a Biennale exhibit.

I unpacked and did some washing, hanging it on the clothesline strung outside the window. The cats on the same level but in the block next door peered at me across their window boxes with looks of mesmerised curiosity. It was about to kill kitty: one of them began investigating ways to get across to me, of which there were none. And a drop of about twenty feet. I ducked back inside giggling. It was a bit ridiculous how delightful all that was for me.

I was in working class Cannaregio, right on the famous bridge, Ponte delle Guglie, that joins the residential neighbourhood to the railway station. The Cannaregio Canal is one of the main access points between the Grand Canal and the lagoon, so *vaporetti* and service craft came and went with blasts of air horns. Barely thirty seconds would go by without another urgent, self-important sounding. Along Rio Terra San Leonardo, the main thoroughfare with which my laneway joined, there were fruit and vegetable stalls, butchers, fishmongers, grocery stores and other general amenities. There were old ladies talking loudly and dogs out for walks. This was not couple Venice. This was residential.

I stepped out for a walk and came across the pasticceria Le Café at Venice's second-largest square, Campo Santo Stefano. Two things I am a sucker for: ice cream and cookies. Boy, was I in the right country. Or wrong, depending on your perspective. Le Café had my favourite Italian biscuit, the *occhi di bue*, or bull's eye, the round, jam-filled shortbread sandwich in apricot and raspberry. I couldn't decide between fillings so I ordered both. And a *caffè lungo*, a longer version of a black espresso. I could have made do with one cookie. But heavens, they were amazing. The pastry was soft but firm enough, not crumbly. They were golden brown, and buttery mouth-watering. And the jam filling was fresh, fruity and chewy. They were made all the better because I consciously enjoyed them. Not so long ago I would have wolfed them down as fast as I could, hoping no one would notice I'd ordered two. Or I would have berated myself with every bite. In my life I had wavered between this 'shovel as fast as you can' mode of eating or despising every bite, or both at the same time.

I did believe my weight issues had not been about what I ate, but how I ate. Likewise the drinking. It was not what I drank, but how. In the great scheme of eating, mine was actually not too bad. But I had made food a confusing mix of enemy and comfort and somehow, in the middle of the two, my body lost the ability to deal with it.

I ate too much dinner. I drank too much at night. It was nighttime, not the food, not the booze, that was at least part of the issue. I hated night. The encroaching darkness in the evening was like the shadow of the devil falling on me. I was going to say the shadow of death, but I didn't fear death. I feared night, and an undefined evil it contained for me. Emptiness was caught up in it somewhere, I just wasn't sure where.

Emptiness. I hated emptiness.

At eight o'clock that night as the sun was going down, I was sitting in a crowded bar by myself. This was the first time I had felt uncomfortable, excruciatingly uncomfortable, about the fact that I was drinking again. I didn't know if it was the bar or the drink. Or me. But I was there because I wanted to change my routine, to embrace a bit of evening. I'd already had dinner at home, then gone out. I was sitting there in that bar and I didn't like it. I felt intensely exposed.

This was not my time. It was not my rhythm. It was someone else's. I was not frightened but I couldn't pretend I was enjoying this. I was here because I thought I should be. And because I was looking for him. Him being my, what, soul mate? Partner? Husband? I kept looking. It was an ingrained, habitual tic, like food and drink became.

I had been doing it constantly on this trip so far. I looked at men by themselves and wondered. Ran the checklist. Moved on to the next one. I didn't know what the motivation was. I would have liked to say it was the need to be loved and to love. But that didn't ring true because, here was the thing: since I had strengthened my connection to God, I had never felt more loved, nor felt more love back.

Was it that I felt embarrassed about being single at forty-six? I hated being pitied. I hated being perceived to have failed at such an enormous part of life's equation.

So what did I need to do to stop this? Why was it that I cared so deeply what people thought? There was something at the core of this and I couldn't see it for the life of me. Body issues. Booze. Food. Being single. Searching for 'the one'. Caring what people thought. Easily swayed from what suited me ... Those things all seemed superficial to me. There had to be something far more immense lurking somewhere.

But I did know that sitting in a bar by myself in Cannaregio was not who I was. It was not. I'd done my tour of duty through bars and nightclubs and as sure as Lord Byron knew he would one day outgrow his days of excess, I, thank God, had long outgrown mine.

When I got my journalism cadetship it was almost by default and against the backdrop of six years of making it onto various shortlists but losing out in the end because I was a hopeless examinee and, back then, in the early 1980s, you would have to pass a general knowledge twenty-questions pop quiz to secure an internship. There'd be a panel of three or four male journalists staring at you as someone fired this very serious version of *Who Wants to be a Millionaire?* at you. I would get stage fright, my brain would freeze and I would fail spectacularly. After wowing them with a tap dance of personality and wit, which is the calling card of the people-pleaser, there would be shrugs of shoulders, shakes of heads, some heartbreaking we-think-you're-terrific-but platitudes and then, ultimately, rejection.

Fortunately, a formidable character at *The Herald and Weekly Times* who had a reputation for hiring Catholics and people who barracked for Collingwood was very supportive of me. I fitted one of the criteria, the Catholic bit. I danced around the second bit because I adored the St Kilda Football Club and always would. (I also failed to mention I was what is kindly termed a failed Catholic ...)

It was before the days when buildings were locked up for security and I would occasionally take the day off school with my mother's blessing, dress myself in a smart outfit I would have spent weeks making on the Singer especially for the moment, jump on the train from Ringwood to Flinders Street and go sit outside this man, Bill Howie's, office.

That is remarkable to me from the vantage point of over twenty-five years later. I had such conviction and determination and no fear at all of seeing him. He was the editor-in-chief of the city's newspapers, *The Sun* and *The Herald*, in his office at the end of the hallway of shiny black and white linoleum tiles and wood-panelled walls that they called mahogany row. I remember the amused look on his face when, after I'd been sitting with his secretary a good while, he would stick his head around the door and say, mock resignedly, 'All right, come in then. Gawd, you've had more returns than Dame Nellie Melba.'

Eventually, he took pity on me. Granted, I had got to the top five for a few years but only four were taken. The poor man, he'd have to face me in his office afterwards. Towards the end of 1984 and in between intakes, the cadet at the HWT radio station, 3DB, resigned. Mr Howie, I think, told the head of the radio newsroom to hire me. I did the interview, did a news-reading audition and passed it particularly well. My mother was an amateur but very good stage actress, trained in speech, a stickler for elocution and correct pronunciation, and of course I loved to read out loud and show off how good I was at it. More to the point, I didn't have to do twenty questions and all was well.

My sister Erin had become the publicist on *Prisoner* and a little show that had just started called *Neighbours*, and after I finished my night shift reading news, I'd sometimes go out on the town with her and a few budding stars. Melbourne began to open up to us. We always laugh that before the Hilton sisters there was Erin and me, without the inheritances—and with a modicum more of modesty.

I was made morning newsreader on 3DB and the 4.15 a.m. starts nearly killed me. I applied to finish my cadetship at ABC Radio and was accepted.

Mr Howie was sad to see me go after such a short time in the HWT building. My dad was happy. He had worked at the ABC also. Unfortunately, this not only meant I was surrounded by a lot of his mates, but also his second wife, who worked there as a typist. It was uncomfortable and weird sometimes, but I was on a career high. I was all over the radio doing live crosses and special reports, and I'd very quickly moved into high-importance reporting.

I was working at Trades Hall covering industrial relations in the days when Norm Gallagher and the Builders Labourers Federation were sticking it to the state government and when nurses would go on strike for days on end. It was riveting. I picked up cigarettes, my first brand being Silk Cut—not a readily available brand in Australia then—because a boy who reported for a newspaper and on whom I had a brief crush smoked them.

The drinking was big. It was what you did.

And then I moved into business reporting, without any thought or consideration. The business round came up. No one senior to me wanted it. It was anathema to the newsroom's then lefty leanings. I put up my hand and got it, leap-frogging from a cadet to a B-grade journalist (which was a good thing: gradings went from D to A) practically overnight.

Newspapers were being bought and sold. Television stations were changing hands. Tycoons were rising on stacks of, in the end, worthless paper. And long boozy lunches were the norm on a gravy train that had no end in sight. I was there and then not. Though I kicked goal after career goal, I lived with this constant, terrifying feeling that I would be found out as not belonging, as not smart enough. I felt like a fraud. I had no interest whatsoever in the business world but I'd been seduced by it because, in the 1980s, there was no more influential place in the journalistic lexicon. Here I was, on a flight of ego's fancy, not from any real motivation or interest. It kept me awake at night, this feeling of being not good enough, not real enough, which I see now was the intuitive knowledge that I had no business being there because it *was not* who I really was. The outside world saw an achiever, a girl on the rise. I saw a person who did not belong, who had fooled everyone, and who any minute now would be found out.

Meanwhile, my sister's social cachet was rising, as she became the person who could bring celebrities to nightclubs. Mine rose with hers. Wherever we went we would get limitless free drinks. There was a time when at one particular club we were drinking only Veuve Clicquot all night long. Complimentary.

Over the next decade, or a bit less, I did lots of weekend, what they called 'recreational', drug using, but it was a lot more than that tippy-toeing phrase implied. Lots of cocaine, lots of ecstasy, some speed and the occasional trip (often inadvertently; it would be mixed into the ecstasy tablet), and a bit of hash, though marijuana and its related products never did sit well with me, like the aforementioned LSD. It was horrible for someone who had lots of things to hide from herself and who needed to hold together a particular persona to function.

One Monday night, spent from the weekend before, I asked our housemate, Julian, a sweet boy from Perth who played bass in a then huge band, to go up the street to Toorak Road and buy us a bottle of wine and some lasagne. As I had every Monday night for probably months, I offered to pay for his share if he'd run the errand.

'Okay,' said Julian. 'But when I get back we're going to sit down and work out how much you've spent this year on drugs, alcohol and buying me dinner when you're messed up like this.' Uh-oh. We did it though. I'd spent over half my wage, a wage that was very good for that time. Half of it. Despite getting a lot of drugs and alcohol for free.

I let American Express cards default though I had a new outfit every Saturday night, and sometimes every Friday night too. I had expensive dinners on other people's credit cards, promising to pay them back but never doing so. I owed friends money and they became not friendly.

I had a succession of cars, cute-looking British things like Austins and Triumphs, but all bombs because I didn't do research or checks and would fall in love with how they looked, then not look after them and drive them till they broke down. Then I would abandon them in the street somewhere, walk away, leave them there till they were towed and sold by the council. I'd ignore the parking fines, not answer the door to the sheriff (till he once came to my workplace, a proud moment), and still manage to hold down a high-responsibility, busy, high-profile job.

A succession of them, that is. I skipped through five jobs in about two years, leaving each one on a whim. Someone would say, 'Hey, *Business Review Weekly* needs a reporter,' and I'd go and do it. *The Herald?* Sure. Channel Nine needs an on-air business reporter—that became me. All this climbing, despite that dreadful insecurity. With each skip, it became more persistent, more troubling.

I was retrenched from Channel Nine when Alan Bond went belly up and I got a job as publications manager for a huge commercial law firm. I had a corner office in a prestigious high-rise and nothing to do because I was a trophy employee and answerable to six partners, all of whom had differing opinions of the job and none of whom would let me actually do anything. So I sat and wrote my first novel, getting my secretary to type it up for me.

They leased for me a BMW 323. I cracked its sump driving over an embankment while on the way home from a nightclub, leaning over to kiss the one-night-stand in the passenger seat. I once lost that expensive car in the city somewhere, because I was driving it while tripping. The city became like a pinball machine with me the ball but somehow reason broke through and I told my four passengers we'd have to seek alternative arrangements for transport to the next nightclub. I found the car behind the art gallery days later, having pieced together clues and vague information from others on the scene. Its windscreen wipers were jammed with parking tickets, which I of course ignored.

I was lucky to be alive. Lucky not to have killed someone. Lucky not to be in jail. Lucky. I mean, *lucky*. On this front, they did not come much luckier than me. I honestly did not know how it happened that I was in Venice, a healthy, relatively sane human being whose only scar from those times, save the emotional ones, was a fairly terrible credit rating.

So we'll go no more a roving
So late into the night ...

Lord Byron's ode to the comedown after Venice's Carnivale conjured up bittersweet reminiscences from that time for me. I did need to remember I met some great people then, had some great times. But I was haunted by the notions of choice and succumbing to weakness. In living this high life, had I forever forsaken any real chance at the more conventional relationships I now craved? Had I lived too much? I'd endlessly drifted into situations and experiences, or at least, felt like I had, not consciously choosing them but I suppose allowing my infirmities and influences to choose for me. It came down to this: was I a victim of my circumstance or a willing participant who had made her bed and now had to lie in it? Or was there a third option, one that included the first two but which was potent with the opportunity to integrate them fully and, in so doing, open up new possibilities?

II

A Sunshiny Day

Ecclesiastes said, that all is vanity—
Most modern preachers say the same, or show it
By their examples of true Christianity ...

Don Juan, Canto VII

Lord Byron's sense of persecution had a push–pull effect on his level of attraction to spirituality, Christianity in particular. He spoke in the House of Lords on civil rights for Roman Catholics in Britain. He described Catholicism, not altogether straight-faced but not altogether facetiously, as 'assuredly the eldest of the various branches of Christianity, what with incense, pictures, statues, altars, shrines, relics and the real presence, confession, absolution—there is something sensible to grasp at.' And he would tell his closest friends he might possibly be devout by the time his life ended. And if the weather was nice. 'I am always most religious on a sunshiny day,' is another of his famously kooky quotes on the subject. At other times, he was critical to the point of causing accusations of atheism, considered a fairly heinous moral transgression in the England of the time in which he lived.

The truth of his spirituality showed in his writing. He had a sense of the divine, a marvellous affinity with God's gifts, especially in the face of nature's bloom. Such was the Romantic poet's way. But few did it with such beauteous gusto as Byron in full flight.

> The morn is up again, the dewy morn,
> With breath all incense, and with cheek all bloom,
> Laughing the clouds away with playful scorn,
> And living as if earth contain'd no tomb,—
> *Childe Harold's Pilgrimage*, Canto III

He saw God in the small, natural things.

But he also often felt forsaken by God and most often troubled by hypocrisy in his name. As someone thought to be the devil himself by his own pious society, he had firsthand experience.

He was, a lot of the time, a man torn between hedonism and mysticism. Even while he was spending his Venetian evenings engaged in feasting and 'fair fucking' as he called it, for a period of time he daily rowed his gondola to the Isola di San Lazzaro to study with the Armenian monks who had colonised it. The Mechitarists were a Christian order exiled from their homeland by the Ottomans. Lord Byron had empathy for their statelessness. He found in their scholarliness welcome cerebral relief from the 'pantaloon humour' of many of his associates. He met a challenge in learning their language, which he described as having a 'Waterloo of an alphabet'. And he had the fallen Christian's love of the Old Testament legends with which Armenia was associated. It was on the Ararat Range in Armenia that the Book of Genesis claimed Noah's Ark came to rest.

The islet's isolation, too, made it an ideal spot for its long-past use as a leper colony, and as a hermitage for Lord Byron, in stark contrast to his other daily outing, a trip to the island of Lido for horse riding.

In physical exercise there was for him communion with nature, and in exercise of the mind and soul connection with the divine. In them he could still feel his realness, when all about him was masks and folly. We all need that. When the storms of the world's distractions batter us, our connections to earth and sky are what anchor us and soothe us after the bruising is done.

Lord Byron would have a hard time galloping his horse along the Adriatic shoreline on Lido these days. Getting past the changing sheds and umbrellas, even on May days, when Lido is still quiet, would be like an Olympic dressage event. The fleshy summer onslaught of June and July would rule it out completely.

Lord Byron came to Lido at the same time most days for a good strong equestrian workout and for swimming in the ocean, his routine leaving him open to looky-loos who knew exactly when they would get a gander at him. Some would come up close and examine him as if he were a museum piece. He handled it okay. In some of those later days he craved the glory of his early success, I suppose, and any attention became good attention.

We all just want to be loved.

Lido is the largest of Venice's islands and the most resort-like, with an old-fashioned beach holiday vibe due to the fact that its eastern extreme faces out to sea with a proper sandy shoreline. It is flat and sprawling and so I did the next best thing to riding a horse on Lido. I rented a bike for a couple of hours, cycling from one end to the other. The sea air did me the world of good, as did the unwitting contribution of the proper cyclist who lapped my no-gears, basket-on-front Hollander and me several times on his high-tech bike. He was wearing white Lycra, and with each lap, he perspired more, thus making his excellent bike-toned derrière more visible through his increasingly diaphanous shorts. I'm no letch, but what a gift, right in front of me like that. And eh, when in *Italia* ... He did have a nice bum.

I returned my bicycle to the rental place and walked down Gran Viale Santa Maria Elisabetta, Lido's main strip where the gaudy Grande Albergo Ausonia & Hungaria with its candy-coloured art nouveau façade pins the place to yesteryear, despite the internet cafés and fast food joints placing the island decidedly in today. I arrived at the *vaporetto* pier and discussed, in my usual mix of charades, monosyllables and *capito-non-capito* coaxing of the same from an official, the next part of my itinerary for the afternoon. I wanted to go to the monastery of San Lazzaro degli Armeni, where Lord Byron had studied with the monks. We established that my desired *vaporetto* was coming in ten minutes. *Grazie mille*, I would go to the toilet across the way in the meantime then.

When I got to the facilities the attendant was in an intense phone conversation and crying loud and uninhibited. She hung up when by the shuffling in my purse it became clear I didn't have the right change. Once I had her attention, I tried to use my charades and monosyllables to console her. But she was fine five seconds after the end of the call anyway. Such is Italy and her emotional openness.

I took the opportunity to straighten myself up a bit and looked in the mirror to discover that, while I was cycling merrily, a bug had met its demise on my forehead, like a billion of its brethren on windshields. The bug was squished and smeared across my shiny, unveiled forehead in plain view as I had my fringe back in a scarf. Why didn't people tell you when you had a dead bug smeared across your face? Maybe the *vaporetto* man did and I missed it. Maybe this is what cheered up the washroom attendant so quickly.

If you're going to be a monk, the monastery of San Lazzaro is a good place to be one. Smack dab in the middle of the Venetian lagoon, it's a graceful conglomeration of orange stucco and green-shuttered lodgings overlooked by a distinctive clock-faced campanile and surrounded by trees, lawn and lavish hot-pink climbing roses that seemed to grow ever bigger before my eyes.

The tour was nice, though not very satisfying. I liked visiting the room where Lord Byron studied. But I got annoyed, as I always do at such things, that there was an Egyptian mummy in the middle of it, a donation from some wealthy Armenian to the monks. It was there apropos of nothing but show and tell.

I left the tour and the monastery and sat on the pier in the late afternoon sun waiting for the *vaporetto* to come back. I was joined by a man, about my age, balding, slicked hair, black architectural glasses, a thin flatness to his mouth, like a frog. He was impeccably dressed, in pressed chinos and a pale-pink polo. He had a leather Armani shoulder bag and a lithe femininity to his gestures. I pegged him gay.

'You did not like the tour?' he asked. His accent was Italian.

'Oh, well, you know, when the Italian version of the commentary about something goes for ten minutes and the English goes for one, you can't help but feel you are missing out on something.'

'Ah.' He shrugged. We sat in silence for a minute.

'Where are you from?'

'Australia.'

'I knew it,' he said, a smile on his face, an animated self-congratulation to his gestures. 'I hear your accent before, inside. Why you come here, to this place? Your family from Armenia?'

'No, just curious,' I said.

'Are you Christian?'

It was a bit like the 'have you ever been married' question for me. It still felt uncomfortable to answer. Because the truth was, I was, though not in any conventional sense. And the word 'Christian' was so loaded.

We were a church-at-Christmas-and-Easter family, though for a while there Erin and I were packed off to mass while everyone else slept in of a Sunday. We'd make our appearance on behalf of the wayward Jamesons, before skedaddling off to 21 Flavours near the clock tower for a milkshake. At some stage when I was very small we must have gone semi-regularly as a family, though, because there was a young parish priest, Father Noonan, who used to be a fixture at parties at our house. (He ended up leaving the priesthood.)

I was all of fifteen when I was home alone at Lavender Street one Friday night watching the movie of *Jesus Christ Superstar* on TV. Strangely, halfway through, that movie awoke in me a deep feeling I didn't understand. I was so moved by the portrayal of Jesus' life, his service and betrayal, I cried inconsolably. What Sunday school could not do, that seventies rock opera certainly did. The crying went on for days in secret, in my bedroom, in the high branches of the willow tree I loved to climb, in the bush behind the Catholic school just down the road where I would ride my bike into solitude, or in a cubicle in the school toilets at lunchtime.

I couldn't talk to anyone. Religion was material for comedy at home. Jesus was the height of non-cool at school. Those

Christian kids, though pleasant enough, were not my bag. Plus, I suspected they would have no empathy at all with me. Hand clapping, weekend camps and good deeds for the neighbourhood elderly had nothing to do with the seismic disturbance at my core. It was baffling and debilitating.

I went up to the church on my bike and knocked on the presbytery door. The housekeeper answered.

'Can I see a priest?' I was sobbing again as soon as I opened my mouth. This alarmed the blue-rinsed little old lady, who said nothing and scurried for assistance, no doubt thinking I was a pregnant teen. I heard some mumbling and whispering, then after a while, a youthful priest came to the door with an expression of apprehension behind a fixed smile.

He invited me into a parlour where a bunch of home-grown roses in a cut crystal vase were losing a battle with the pervasive smell of fried meat and Gravox.

I blurted out my story with a sense of camaraderie and relief. At last, a person who understood, who felt the same. 'All the things he did for us, then what they did to him,' I said between sodden hiccups and gasps. Yet I was worried. I had put myself in a gap between my daily life and this new one, whatever it was. That was a feeling that would come back to me when I first walked into AA. But this man in front of me, he understood how my heart broke for Jesus. He could tell me what to do with myself from here on in.

I looked into his face to receive my guidance. I saw terror, legs tightly crossed, hands tightly clasped in his lap and an expression that telegraphed his internal dialogue: 'Okay, Father, hold it together. Try not to look alarmed. We were told in the seminary about hysterical teenage girls. All you need to do is remember what you were taught, but dear God, what is she on about?'

The passion that was erupting inside me meant it took a moment to comprehend what was happening. But soon enough, it was clear to me that he and I were not going to be the thirteenth and fourteenth apostles. 'Go home and read the Bible,' he said with that same fixed smile, trying to force a gentle, benevolent tone and instead sounding patronising and like he had an urgent need to be elsewhere.

The spiritual rush had been corked.

I rode home feeling like an idiot, hoping no one would find out that I'd been up at the church voluntarily talking to a priest. A priest! I'd done something murky, shameful, something so derisible and disloyal to the beliefs and values of my family and friends. The person I could be had betrayed the person I needed to be. Again. I didn't give Jesus another thought. I'd forgotten about the whole thing by breakfast the next day.

Knowing what I know now, it looked like a very powerful moment of spiritual awakening. But what would a fifteen-year-old from Ringwood, Victoria, have done with such a state of being in 1978 anyway? Joined the convent? If the priest's reaction was any indication, this was not the way forward for me.

My reconnection came on my first visit to Italy, after the magazine job went belly up. And it arose after a week of steeping in Rome's vividness. I had gone to the train station to buy a ticket to Florence. I was walking back towards my hotel when I saw the basilica of Santa Maria degli Angeli across the road from Rome Termini. I didn't know anything about it but there was a sign outside explaining how this orange brick, crumbly, near-ruin of a building was originally built as Roman baths and had been appropriated by the Catholic church and given its current interior in the sixteenth century. I stepped inside and found an altogether different environment where the Renaissance had had its way. It was such a shocking contrast. This was amongst

Michelangelo's last works. The magnitude of inspiration in the marble and mosaics caused my body to convulse in a way I had hitherto not known art could engender. I sat down in the nearest pew, in total awe. And then I settled into the magnificence and sat in true, unadulterated wonder. It was the singularity of state you hope to find in meditation. There was nothing between my soul and the essence of what had been created there. And I knew about divine inspiration then.

It was like the end of a long joke, the punch line being 'but you knew that all along'. I had pursued New Age leaders, gone to a Sai Baba ashram in Sydney, flirted with the teachings of another Hindu guru, read up on Buddhism, learned Tibetan meditation, consulted the I-Ching, runes and every spiritual practitioner I could lay my hands on, only to find out that the bloke in the Friday night movie was my guru.

The challenge had been how to integrate that into everyday life. It would take my crisis, when I realised I could no longer drink the way I did, for me to discover the place of the Christ energy in my life. It was everything and nothing all at once. Nothing had changed, but everything had. Life went on, but now I understood, I had support always. And I always had had it. I'd now opened up an opportunity for myself to call on it. To experience it in an understandable way.

I think that's what gives our crises meaning: the moment at which they reintroduce us to what we knew all along. In that, even during my darkest days, I considered myself very lucky.

And so on this, my third trip to Italy, there at the *vaporetto* stop on San Lazzaro, to the man's question of whether I was Christian or not, I simply answered, 'Yes.' That in itself felt like a significant achievement in claiming my power: to say it and not be afraid of the assumptions of others that might arise as a result.

'Would you like to eat with me tomorrow?'

'Sure,' I said. A meal out with a gay Italian in Venice might be fun.

Not that I was short on opportunities for food outside the home. Five minutes from my apartment towards San Marco was Nobile Pasticceria. Their *marmalata*, a flaky, buttery croissant, or *cornetto* as the Italians called it, filled with marmalade, was pure genius. And then there was the Gelateria Leonardo; it should have been criminalised. The damn place was right on my corner. I'd walk down the stairs from my front door, down the alleyway, and into the tiny Campo San Leonardo, and there it was. Right there on the corner with a very popular pizza place on the other corner, so it was just as well I'm not all that into pizza. I had Gelateria Leonardo's *limone* my first visit. It was bitter and creamy and gelatinous and generally unbelievable. Their *fragola*, strawberry, caused delirium, popping with fruit and the sweetness of summer, and they did a yoghurt and honey that would have knocked my socks off were I wearing any. Their vanilla was strange and tastebud tickling and I am not a chocolate ice cream person usually but theirs had a nostalgic balance to it, not too rich, but mild and soothing, like you might have got as a kid when you had your tonsils out.

So no, not short of good food. But company, that was a whole other issue.

12

The Bells of Venezia

Here's a sigh to those who love me,
And a smile to those who hate;
And whatever sky's above me,
Here's a heart for every fate.

To Thomas Moore

Lord Byron had a great big 'heart for every fate', an openness and
a willingness to move forward. Even though the past dragged
on him, he did not allow those ropes to hold him still, choosing
instead to ride the tides of fortune and fate like the sailboats
he so loved bearing up on a windy Lac Leman. Sometimes his
kinesis was about avoiding boredom. The pursuing forces of
expectation and responsibility would propel him further.
When they caught up with him, he could display confronting
callousness and a ready punch. Even then he was giving full
expression to the evolution of his being. For better or worse, he
was not afraid to go with life.

But he would have been a handful for those who loved
him, or sought to be loved by him. That's for sure. Likewise
for those who hated him and whom he hated, because he was
impossible to ignore.

His final years in Venice were marked by fateful changes,

for him and those closely connected to him. In early 1818 he was negotiating with Claire Clairmont over bringing their illegitimate daughter, Allegra, only one year old, to live with him in Italy. He was resigned to the fact that Lady Byron was never going to let him near their child, Ada. Allegra seemed his only hope at some sense of dynasty. His wish came true purely through the fact of Percy Shelley's ill health. Physicians had suggested the consumptive poet seek warmer climes than England. Claire and Allegra came along with Shelley and Mary, and when Allegra was on the Continent, Lord Byron sent for her. By eighteen months old, she had fully joined the circus at Palazzo Mocenigo, where her papa doted on her, amidst the human and animal menagerie. She quickly began speaking Venetian and learned even more quickly to swim, when her proudly amphibious father, who had famously swum the length of the Grand Canal, threw her over the side of his gondola. And sometimes she'd be suddenly packed off to the home of friends for periods of time when his parental attention span ran out.

It was around this time that Lord Byron began *Don Juan*, his tour de force and, in many ways, his downfall in England. He was still the most talked about man in London. His poetry still sold well. Now here came the first stanzas of this epic, going where no man of his standing had gone before: into a place where women were sexual aggressors, and older women towards younger men at that, where society was satirised more directly than ever before, important living poets and peers were named and shamed, and where a man openly took pot shots at his ex-wife. There was dark, cutting humour and explicit sex, bawdiness and bad temper. There was only so much of that 1800s Britain could take—and over the next five years there would be seventeen cantos to come, some over 200 stanzas long.

The decisions we make, the choices we take; we are the sum of them. At any given moment in time, there are a million directions we can go. Perhaps all that is asked is that in making the choices we do, we commit to them as fully as we can, and try not to harm anyone along the way. But it's so hard to do that, especially as first and foremost we must try to not harm ourselves. To balance the needs and wants of those around us with our own, that is a trapeze act, and the tightrope on which we delicately step is a thin line running between self-respect and selfishness.

Venice can be so terrifically in your face when you are dealing with it at the mass tourism end. I had thought that to truly enjoy Venice you needed money and lots of it. I had believed there were two Venices, the one akin to Lord Byron's, albeit a modern take on that, where people moored insanely expensive private cruising craft adjacent to San Marco in the Giudecca Canal and flitted from villas to parties to galleries in private runabouts. The other Venice was where tourists trudged the same old overcrowded paths between San Marco and the railway station, stopping in shops selling trinkets made in China, getting overcharged for coffee, sandwiches and cheap wine any self-respecting quaffer wouldn't touch at home.

Now I knew that there was a third Venice, the one where the working Venetians lived and co-existed in the quiet backstreets of Cannaregio, frequenting streets and *piazze* and *trattorie* that the tourists hardly got to, even the high-end ones. I liked this Venice very much, but I felt it was closed to me, a visitor, and fair enough too. Subjected to a swarm of tourists coming relentlessly, day in, day out, all year, every year (even the Biblical plagues had an end, but not this one), I didn't think I'd be particularly welcoming in my peaceful little neighbourhood either. Venetians had to preserve a sense of community somehow and somewhere. It would be unbearable otherwise.

Claudio, the bespectacled gay Italian, sent me a text message. Could I make lunch? At a place called Linea d'Ombra in Dorsoduro. *Si*, that would be lovely. It was such a delightful day.

Reaching the edge of the Giudecca Canal, I was struck by the peace there. The air. The way life went on, boats chugged, people strolled—only without the craziness of San Marco. Two perfectly formed Palladian churches stared over from the island of Giudecca. The Chiesa dei Gesuati o Santa Maria del Rosario stared back at them. I was early so I went in and found it a wonderfully cohesive place compared to the riot some of these churches could be. It still thrilled me that you could walk in off the street somewhere in Venice and be confronted by the work of Tiepolo or Tintoretto. Just like that. I continued along towards Punta della Dogana, the triangular building at the end of the boardwalk with my favourite of Venice's monuments, twin Atlases upholding a globe with Fortune perched atop, shining newly golden due to the property being renovated by a French art collector and fashion tycoon. Workmen were applying the finishing touches to the building, in time for Biennale. I looked at my watch. It was lunchtime.

Linea d'Ombra had bright-white thick linen tablecloths, snappy-looking waiters and a modern vibe with cleanly elegant furniture. It reeked of expensive and wonderful—unlike some of the neighbouring restaurants with the typical red and white checked tablecloth, waistcoated-waiters-type deal that lured in tourists. I spotted my gay date, Claudio, at the best table in the house, right at the water's edge on the pontoon that floated outside the restaurant. It directly faced one of Palladio's perfect churches, while to the left of it you could see the Grand Canal, a flotilla of billionaire boats and all about the sparkling expanse of the Giudecca Canal.

'*Ciao, bella,*' Claudio said, standing up and kissing me on both cheeks. He was wearing a cravat under a very expensive-looking white shirt. I was awfully glad I'd made an effort and had popped my Birkenstocks in my bag and changed into a pair of heels on the stoop of the church. He pulled my chair out and motioned to the waiter to pour me some wine.

I got Lord Byron's Venice then. The effortlessness of life lived well in one of the most ravishing places in the world. The day was not too hot, the breeze was soft, the boats came and went, glasses tinkled and waiters glided about. And yes, I had a glass of wine, and this was exactly how I had hoped it would one day be: in moderation and for the pleasure of it. There was none of the manic yes–no carry on. I thought it would be nice, so I had it. And it was.

'So, tell me, where do you live in Australia?'

'Sydney,' I told him. 'My family is from Melbourne.'

'Are you single?'

'Ah, yes!' I said, as if I was saying, as I would have in my seventies schoolyard, 'derr'. 'I live in Sydney—the gay capital? There's a lot of single women in Sydney.' I laughed, expecting some recognition on his part. He didn't laugh and no recognition was forthcoming.

'I have a friend in Melbourne,' said Claudio. 'He lives there with his wife. I went there and stayed with them. I want to live there. He is my best friend.'

I wondered what the wife thought of that relationship.

Claudio told me he was a sommelier, in town working on some large catering job for Biennale. He had been to Venice many times before. This was why he'd taken the trip out to San

Lazzaro. It was one of the few parts of the lagoon city he'd never been to. 'Last time I was here I was with my girlfriend. But we were close to breaking up. She did not want to do any of the little trips.'

Girlfriend. Well, sometimes these Italian men were hard to read, but not that hard. Surely. I had one of the world's most finely tuned gaydars.

'Do you like to do little trips in Australia? I saw the Great Barrier Reef and I went to the Gold Coast. I liked it very much. The Palazzo Versace hotel on the Gold Coast, oh, so beautiful. Have you been there?' He continued on in this way for a while, the Barossa, the Opera House ... 'And I love Australian music. My favourite is Kylie Minogue.'

Okay. The gaydar may have its off days, but Kylie love coming from a man can only mean one thing. And not that there was anything wrong with that. I just wondered why he felt he had to make with the girlfriend thing.

'In Australia, you are very lucky. Your taxation is very low. In Italy, we are taxed so highly. My dream is to open an *enoteca* in Melbourne. It would be very good. I would open it with my friend.'

The day rolled by, more talk about Australia, more talk about the friend, more excitement about the Australian taxation system. I didn't mind. He was sweet, though he was either in denial or intent on putting on a show for whatever reasons. It was a perfect Venetian summer afternoon and I was at ease and enjoying myself. Dessert came.

'So, Julietta,' he said, taking my hand in his. 'I love you. Do you love me?'

'You ... I'm sorry, what?'

'I love you. You must check out of your hotel and come and stay at my hotel.'

Somehow I found myself playing along with this. And when he kissed me goodbye, which was one of the worst, most passionless kisses of my life, I knew for sure that he did not love me, he loved the idea of Australia and its superior tax system. And quite possibly his male friend in Melbourne.

But instead of being an adult and telling him, er, how about no for a good answer, I said okay, I will come and stay with you.

I went back to my apartment and wrote a note to Claudio explaining that I had decided to leave Venice early and thanks for the memories. I went to his hotel, handed it to the front desk as quickly as I could and skulked away.

And then I walked into the crush of San Marco's madness. It was only ten minutes later that he began texting me relentlessly with protestations of love and imploring me to come back to his hotel and take up where we left off. And it confused me. It really did.

It had been years since a man had even looked like he wanted me that badly, had told me he loved me and had begged for my company. Even though I knew his motivation was suspect to say the very least, my last relationship had been with that man who could not use the L word.

The next day, I was halfway up the Grand Canal to the west, sitting on a pier dangling my legs. It was midday and the churches chimed their daily herald of high noon. Claudio was still texting me, begging me not to leave. From where I sat, it was like all the bells in the world were ringing. There was a chill in the air and rain clouds on the horizon. The weekend was going to be wet.

Twenty minutes later I was in a toilet cubicle by the Rialto Bridge, broken down in a way I hadn't been since I first stopped drinking. I was a mess of snot and tears and screams I kept silent because I didn't want to alarm all the holidaymakers in cubicles alongside me.

I had to be me now, I couldn't be anyone else. Enough of putting someone else's needs before mine. My needs mattered. They did. That kid who had put all that emotion in the box in the face of her parents fighting, she deserved better than this, way better than men using her as tickets to Australia. *Be yourself. Just be you.* I thought I heard an angel's voice.

My head rose above the water. The emotional tide stopped still and I was compelled to wade out. Just walk. Just move. I slid my sunglasses on and pushed myself out into the crowded street. Japanese tour groups following women with umbrellas in the air, fathers with toddlers on their shoulders, teenagers giggling and jostling, Indian touts trying to lure customers into restaurants, they came at me. I saw the doorway to a church and ducked into it, San Giovanni Elemosinario. I sat in a pew, trying to catch my breath. The art was astounding. Titian had painted the portrait of Saint John the Merciful above the altar. The image was of the saint handing alms to the poor. These spaces, these people, they had come to mean sweet solace to me. I asked for my alms. A sign, maybe. Something. Some help.

I left the church, and trying to make my way back to my apartment I got lost. In the state of me, that lost was like being in the depths of the Amazon. The Venetian landscape wrapped around me tight. I gave up on my map, moreover my ability to read it. But I had the thought: if I could keep getting glimpses of the Grand Canal on the left, then I would know I was on track.

The Grand Canal would disappear. And those lanes and bridges would double back on themselves without me realising they had. The Grand Canal would reappear on the right.

Just when it seemed the labyrinth was endless and I would wander bewildered and dazed forever, I unexpectedly came out onto the Grand Canal at the San Tomà *vaporetto* stop. It looked directly onto Lord Byron's Palazzo Mocenigo. Completely without design, there I was opposite his balcony. The sun came out and sent the water into sparkles. Such was my beacon, my way forward on this journey, popping up right when I needed him.

Be yourself. Just be you. Lord Byron had never been anything but. It was time I tried me on for size.

I texted Claudio and told him to stop contact. Enough was enough. And he did. But you know what? I was sad. I missed his flowery Italian entreaties. I didn't miss him, though.

On my last full day in Venice I decided I would go to a cute little neighbourhood *campo* which I had passed through a couple of times and loved. Go for a bit of breakfast as my outing of the day, before attending to some business and packing, as I was leaving Venice the next morning. I couldn't remember the name of the *campo* but figured I'd walked through it three times, I could find it.

I set off thinking that I had finally fallen in love with Venice, on a deeper level than only for her beauty. I loved how you could overhear the local dialect, the people saying '*che, che*' in place of '*si, si*'. I'd grown to love the loud blasts of the horn as the water buses approached the Ponte delle Guglie and manoeuvred the sharp dogleg underneath it with what looked like the waterborne equivalent of slamming on the handbrake and letting the rear-wheel skid do all the work. And with absolutely no view of what was coming the other way, I loved how extraordinary it was that they didn't have collisions on a daily basis. I loved that whole movie-set thing Venice had; step behind the tourism scenery and there was another, totally different life going on. And I loved the blue the sky went at night for the hour or two after the sun had disappeared.

I thought I could maybe live there for a while. If I gave it time, I could crack this nut. Maybe I would come back and do that.

And then I got lost. Again. An infuriating, exhausting, hungry lost. Set out in Venice without knowing exactly where you are going? And without breakfast in your stomach? Big mistake. Venice picked me up and slapped me one last time. She was like all the men I had ever loved, like Lord Byron himself: radiant, powerful, alluring, aloof, inconsistent, selfish and absolutely non-committal. No good could come from trying to love her in the conventional way one loved a city, through familiarity, intimacy, and how it made you feel about yourself. If you chose to love her, you had to do so on her terms. Yes, a lot like those men I'd loved. Maybe that was what I had gone there to learn. If I was ever to have fulfilling love, I had to see where it was not possible. It was not possible in trying to love a city like Venice and have it love me back.

I ended up back in the neighbourhood where I had my coffee every day. On my second *caffè lungo*, a man slid up from his spot two tables away. We chit-chatted enough to ascertain that he was Carlo and I was Julietta and that neither of us spoke the language of the other. Then he asked me for sex. We may have had no language skills in common but some messages transcended. As did his 'But I am such a fine specimen of a man, how could you say no?' reaction to me knocking him back, which I am of course paraphrasing because it was in Italian. But like the language of *amore*, the language of prideful indignation also transcended.

This was not how it was supposed to be. Where was Gregory Peck on a Vespa, picking me up *Roman Holiday* style? Had Saint

Anthony, to whom I'd sent a very clear message of my romantic desires, muddled my order at the mystic checkout? Or was it me who'd muddled it? Was I destined to be single after all? Did this all come back to that: accepting my life, a lonesome traveller whose advantages were many, just different to the things I'd once expected they'd be?

I paid up, said '*Ciao*' to the luckless Lothario and went for a final Venetian walk to a fragrance shop that I had found days earlier behind Lord Byron's *palazzo*. I wanted to buy a thank-you gift for Nina, whom I would be seeing in Verona the next day. She had organised an apartment for me, and was picking me up at the railway station to take me to it. I'd decided on a week in Verona. Lord Byron had not spent any real length of time there, but it was still the Veneto. I felt my time in Venice was done and so many people I had spoken to thought highly of Verona.

Plus my name is Julietta. Though I groaned each of the many times someone made a Romeo joke upon hearing that, I had this thought that maybe he was there. I was torn between knowing that I should stop looking and needing to remain hopeful and open. Verona was calling me.

13

Verona

She then surveys, condemns but pities still
Her dearest friends for being dressed so ill.

One has false curls, another too much paint,
A third—where did she buy that frightful turban?
A fourth so pale she fears she's going to faint,
A fifth's look's vulgar, dowdyish and suburban ...

Beppo

Lord Byron may have had the face of an Adonis and the charisma of well, Lord Byron, but his physical insecurities could debilitate his emotional growth like a teenager addicted to diet pills.

His foot, of course, was the main cause, and the thin calf attached to it. In his early years they were a source of physical torture, as doctors attempted to train them into normalcy with all manner of painful and useless contraptions. There's nothing quite like enduring prodding and poking and insensitive medical prattle to instil in a young person a sense of being subnormal.

One of the real triumphs of Lord Byron's story is how, though he could not run, jump or kick a ball, he found physical activities in which to excel: swimming, especially. He was so competitive, both as a result of and despite his disability.

Though not well off, his mother spent disproportionately on expensive cloth and top tailors for fine trousers to cover up and distract from his unusual leg, beginning Lord Byron's lifelong penchant for finery. In Venice, his look would become its most dandified, though dangerously, sexily so, with gold chains and open puffy shirts, long hair and boots. (Where would Jim Morrison and Michael Hutchence have been were it not for that role model?)

Without the foot and its associated insecurities, without the foppish costumes, without the brooding sense of being damaged, Lord Byron would not have become the figure he was.

The sum of Lord Byron's myriad aspects was and is the legend. Without the ego and vanity born of compensation there would be no Byron. Was it the healthiest life? No. Would he have created even more glorious work had he lived long enough to undo all that damage? Maybe. But that question is futile. His life was what it was, meaningful.

A person who brandishes their neuroses as their means of expression may not find the completion of someone who sheds theirs. But we who attempt the shedding need the brandishers, especially the arse-out, honest ones whose stories we can access. Because of Byron's poems and prolific letter writing, his tale stands astonishingly complete. Like Shakespeare's flawed heroes—Hamlet, Lear, Richard—he is our shadow. Our own dark secrets. From flawed heroes we have much to learn about ourselves, if we can drop judgment and draw near.

Nina picked me up from Verona train station and drove me into the centre of town where we passed a really big wow: an enormous red medieval castle, the wonderful Castelvecchio, once a military hive, now an art gallery. We made our way down busy Via Cavour, lined with Renaissance *palazzi*, little bars and restaurants, a twelfth-century church undergoing restoration, and a Fitness First gym. Nina stopped her car outside a *palazzo* with a big wooden arch of a door. There was a petite, well-coiffed *signora* in neat pedal pushers and a crisp shirt waiting for us. 'Ah, there's the *contessa*,' said Nina.

My first Italian *contessa*! I'd met an Italian princess in Tuscany the year before, and now a *contessa*! And I was renting from her! Wow. I was so impressed. And also dismayed at myself. I was dressed okay, but that morning I'd travelled across from Venice by train. I tended not to wear my finery riding the European rails. Not that I owned finery. How these Italian women—and men—made it look so easy to be chic was beyond me. In Australia I was often considered overdressed. In Italy, Verona in particular, I may as well have been in pyjamas.

My piece of the *palazzo* was the garret, a real garret, right in the roof. At least half the floor space was uninhabitable because of the angle of the ceiling. But who cares, it was a garret and it was heaven. The bath was tucked under the slope, so you couldn't stand up even if you wanted to. The whole place looked out along the higher wall onto the central courtyard and across rooftops towards Verona's famous Arena, an artfully restored Roman Colosseum-style structure, much loved and used by the locals for everything from opera to Italian pop shows. The *contessa* had agreed to let me stay for a fee within my budget as a favour to Nina.

'November 7, 1816. I have been over Verona. The amphitheatre is wonderful—beats even Greece. Of the truth of Juliet's story they seem tenacious to a degree, insisting on the fact—giving a date (1303), and showing a tomb. It is a plain, open, and partly decayed sarcophagus, with withered leaves in it, in a wild and desolate conventual garden, once a cemetery, now ruined to the very graves. The situation struck me as appropriate to the legend, being blighted as their love.'

So Lord Byron wrote to his friend and biographer, Thomas Moore. When he was in Verona, he had yet to visit Rome. I thought that, had he, he might have noted the Veronese Arena, which he referred to as the amphitheatre, to be even better than the Colosseum. Wow. It was so very wow. Made all the more wow by the fact that it was surrounded by a postcard-perfect *piazza* with rows and rows of outdoor diners basking in its glory. Wow.

Verona did not need Juliet's legend. It was the most romantic of cities anyway. Wow.

Nina had taken me on a greatest hits walk around the *centro storico* and I was saying 'wow' every thirty seconds. Which wasn't good. Someone had told me the word was considered a bit déclassé in these northern parts and one thing I had noticed about Verona, apart from its extraordinary architectural and topographical wonders, was its classiness. Central, historical Verona at least, is the utopian Italian city, all handsome, sartorially splendid people, effortlessly enjoying an elegant life amidst the most pleasing buildings against a hilly verdant background. The Adige River snakes through the city, an S running west to east, giving Verona the unfair advantage of riverbanks and their associated charms every which way. Layers of history survived World War II, despite Verona's proximity to Germany and its forces marching right to the doorstep. Medieval churches and monuments built by the Scaligeri, a dynasty that ruled for hundreds of years before submitting to Milan and Venice, comprise a magnificent architectural legacy. The Venetians added their lions, fortifications and Renaissance *palazzi*. And that's not even factoring in the Romans, remnants of whom remain not only in the Arena but also in Teatro Romano, the garden-enmeshed ruins of which date from the first century BC. There are cobbled streets full of elegant shops, little corners of secret local charm and an obvious pride in all of it. If Verona were a woman, she would be well bred, well groomed, well dressed, impossibly comely and rather vain. Much like quite a few of the women who live there.

Nina was an Australian transplanted to Verona, so she ticked all the boxes except the vanity bit. But when she picked me up at the train station, immediately I noticed she had on the most eye-catching set of orange coral jewellery, chunky statement pieces that tied in with her bag, expensive shoes and perfectly stylish garments. I was not five minutes in her company when I could no longer resist commenting on the bling.

'It's our uniform,' she said. 'You're undressed in Verona if you aren't wearing any jewellery.'

In Veronese terms, I was not in pyjamas. I was naked.

The city had me in a festive mood. After Nina left me I decided to keep walking. Up a cobbled street running parallel to a stretch of the river, I spied a corner store with a queue out the door. This was a sight that could only mean one thing at 4.30 on a Thursday afternoon in Italy: excellent gelato. I joined the line. The gelateria was in a pokey cave-like space with the counter arching around one wall and the line of customers following it in one door and out another. The man who was serving was clearly proud of his produce. When I ordered in something resembling Italian, and put my money in the tray on the counter as I was supposed to, he nodded at me like a pleased primary school teacher. I had banana, bursting with fruit, and yoghurt *con fragola*, with strawberry, that was sweet and tangy and tastebud popping. Best. Gelato. Ever. *Mamma. Mia.*

From the gelateria I strolled. It was so nice to stroll. I didn't find I could stroll in Venice or Rome. Or at least, I hadn't thought to. Venice was a running of the gauntlet between sights and Rome was a serious walk. Verona was smaller and more laid back.

It was strolling along that I found myself at Piazza delle Erbe at *apertivo* time. Piazza delle Erbe is the main square in Verona, a conglomeration of ages and styles that comes together cohesively, overseen by Torre Lamberti, an 84-metre-high tower of history, begun in the twelfth century, completed in the fifteenth, its clock face added in the nineteenth. The market was closing up and the dogs were out for walks, beneficently allowing their owners to come along for the jaunt. It was such a seductive time of the day. Everyone seemed carefree and content. I sat down at an outdoor café, ordered a glass of wine and people-watched for an hour.

The combination of expensive timepieces, tennis bracelets and tattoos on those *belle donne* of Verona was a breathtakingly audacious fashion choice, especially en masse. If you needed any evidence that Verona had two football teams, well, it looked like WAG central. I watched tables full of these amazingly groomed and bedecked women drink their spritz, the local tipple of choice, trading an apparently rehearsed warmth with each other as their own mothers nursed adorably dressed *bambini* who chomped on the fat green olives put on the tables to accompany cocktails. Honestly, I had not seen such a fabulous parade of watches outside the opening pages of the US *Vogue* September issue.

A husband arrived carrying a salmon-pink newspaper. He had perfect hair, great bone structure, natty glasses and an excellent suit, and he kissed everyone except his wife. She looked slightly awkward with him. I thought his watch was a Rolex. I'd be uncomfortable too, married to a man like that.

At breakfast in a café the next day there was a woman, impeccably dressed in that very conservative, new moneyed way. Crisp white shirt with double cuffs. Navy blue jeans secured with a navy and white belt. Hogan trainers. Neat shoulder-length brown hair. A ton of gold jewellery. After the initial pang of wishing I had packed one of my white shirts, which by the way, I hardly ever wore at home, there was an unfamiliar settling, an acceptance that I could not look like everyone. I could not be all things to all people.

I'd tried. In the mid-1980s clothing, not alcohol, was my compulsion. Shopping for clothes was still entirely irresistible to me. I loved fashion, of a sort. I loved finding things that expressed me. But back then I went through a lengthy phase of buying clothes and changing into them in a public toilet somewhere on the way to work. There were a few shops I favoured, all outlets, open early and on my way to the office. Outlets, so it wasn't so bad, was it? Except for the volume. A lot of cheap soon became expensive. But I was so uncomfortable with myself I could not stop doing it. I would only be able to start my day if I was wearing something new.

I stopped when I moved jobs and had an earlier start. But for many, many years, I had still compulsively bought and thrown out, bought and thrown out.

There were those times in the late 1980s when I would insist on having something new to wear to the nightclubs every Saturday night. My girlfriends, my sister and I would go shopping on Chapel Street and ask the assistants to put the purchases through in multiple amounts, each under fifty dollars, which was the point at which purchases needed to be phone-authorised. Those days of manual credit card transactions meant my plastic was consistently over the limit. I even had an ATM card confiscated by one bank because I had worked out that on weekends it took their computers a while to catch up to what had been transacted. I would put my account into the red regularly.

It was the same animal as the drinking beast. The same one as the food. For a long time, I could not say no to myself. That thing needing to be filled up. Lord Byron had filled his up with sex.

I was having a hard time saying no to the Gelateria Ponte Pietra. Every afternoon, I went back. His handmade ice cream was the stuff I knew I would think about every day for the rest of my gelato-loving life. I'd had all kinds of berry flavours, cherry, citrus, my standard banana, but this was no ordinary banana, and then some intriguing choices like *zaffrino*, or saffron. Sweet, fragrant, with an unexpected richness, I fell for it like a junkie. But it was one of the gelato man's one-offs. I never got to have it again. Except in my dreams.

Both Lord Byron and I loved to swim. Verona has an outdoor Olympic swimming pool that runs along a section of the old Roman wall. It was a phenomenal location for some exercise. After my laps, I watched a group of newly pubescent boys and girls play spin-the-bottle. There were four skinny, smooth-skinned girls and one curvy, bigger and looser-fleshed girl. This stuff does not change, I thought. She was me in 1976. I watched her, amid the giggles and pecks of kisses of her friends, as mechanical as those meaningless hugs teenagers give each other, her body language running the gamut of discomfort from the knees pulled to the chest, to lying down on her stomach, to pretending to snooze, to looking into the distance with disinterest. She'd clearly told them she wasn't playing their silly game. And though the boys said the Italian version of 'Eew, girl germs' no matter who they kissed, I was sure that in her head, if the bottle had landed on her, they would have recoiled in horror or run screaming or said something dreadfully cruel and life-threatening.

I knew exactly what was going on. Our pool at Ringwood, the Fred Dwerryhouse Swimming Centre, looked the same as the Verona pool—save the Roman wall. Same big lawns, sparkling big blue pool. Same too, was the vulnerability of being almost naked with your schoolmates; as excruciating, or exciting, or both. I spent countless hours at the pool with my skinny, tanned girlfriends, all in the cool group like I'm sure these kids were, feeling so bad about myself.

Poor little thing. I wanted to tell her not to spend the next thirty years of her life feeling that way. The girl at that Verona pool—and me.

After all, later that day I saw a woman in a Pucci mini-dress and with a massive beauty queen blow-dry, toned legs and jewelled gladiator sandals riding by on a bicycle. Crazy stunning. But guess what? We passed by the same group of men, who did not react to her but did to me. Italians like a little curve. Trophy was in the eye of the beholder. In this country, a juicy woman would turn a head every time. That was one of the many reasons I loved Italy.

I bought a ticket to The Killers at Verona's Roman amphitheatre. A whim but a good one, I thought. It just so happened that I was walking along and saw a poster announcing that they were playing the Arena. I was on my way to the Arena to do the touristy thing, the guided tour, etc. When I saw the poster, I decided against the tour, did some investigating through a series of interviews—charades, *capito-non-capito*, now combined with a smattering of Italian—with people who

I thought might know where I could get a ticket (policemen, parking inspectors, street sweepers), and then I walked in the vague direction of the box office. Amazingly (particularly if you knew the various sets of conflicting directions I was given during my research), I found it. I asked, 'The Killers, *uno, numerato.*' One assigned seat, in other words. I had picked this up while I waited in the queue.

'*No,*' she said. Then, '*Uno momento.*' She clacked about on the computer and came back with the news—in English now—that a batch of tickets had just been released. 'Very beautiful tickets,' she said.

And so I went to see the band at that spectacular first-century AD Roman amphitheatre. In the past I had been annoyed and fascinated by the singer, Brandon Flowers, because he had plenty of interesting things to say, among them that The Killers would be the biggest band in the world, which I found at the time audacious and affronting. But when I saw them I was struck by his genuineness. You always know when you see a band live whether or not their art is coming from that soul level. Who was I to doubt their singer's convictions about his destiny?

I was beginning to realise that anything was possible in this life. When I stripped Lord Byron down to his core, I thought he was living his truth, living authentically and, though he could be a braggart at times, the enduring appeal of his art was testimony to his authenticity. Regardless of the noise that surrounded him, when he created, he channelled divine inspiration.

Pop music was pop music, but I was reminded of that genuineness at the amphitheatre.

*

After a good afternoon of writing in my garret, I walked down the road to my gelateria. I lined up, waited my turn, told the man, '*Uno cono, due gusti, banana e mango.*' I was figuring the fruity ones would keep me from getting fat. I took my ice cream to the Ponte Pietra, Verona's most beloved bridge, which had been blown to smithereens by the Germans. The Veronese had pieced it together again painstakingly from the original materials, scavenged from the river. I stood watching the Adige River draining its melted snow cargo into the Adriatic. Halfway up the bridge two men were playing piano accordion accompanied by a boy of maybe ten on violin. They were good. I chucked them a couple of euro when I finished my ice cream. The Roman ruins in the distance, the black storm clouds rolling across, it was a memorable moment.

As I walked back I practised my bad Italian in a salumeria and a fruit shop, then stopped for a vino at Cantina Buglioni, which was like Cheers. Everybody knew everyone else. I wanted to go home to be cosy and write. But I did have to be out here for a while. How was he going to find me if I was not?

A blue-eyed, dimpled four-year-old called Illya flirted with me. He asked in Italian if I was a mamma. Then he asked if I was married. At least it wasn't 'Have you ever been … ?'

A daytime-soap-handsome man came and sat opposite me. They were communal tables but there were plenty of others free. '*Ciao, bella,*' he said casually, then read the paper and had his drink. He was ridiculously good looking, tanned to the point of showing a vanity that would never allow my kind to be his.

I went back to my notebook and to enjoying my glass of wine as much as I could. The Italians did it so well. It was a ritual here, a delicate note that they hit of enjoying the drink while honouring its potency. Respecting it. I had seen some men attempting to paddle rapids where the Adige ran under the Ponte Pietra. They paddled furiously but kept getting pushed back. It was a pointless battle. The river was always going to win if they attacked it hell-for-leather like that. I think they knew it, because when they went up the side, close to the bank, showing awareness of the river's force and where it was safe to paddle, they made headway. Wine had become like that for me. I loved its nuances, its mysterious aliveness. And I did not want to be a stranger to that. I thought it could enrich me but I needed to respect it. Like any hazardous hobby, I had to play by the rules.

There was an inner place where I still didn't trust myself with this. But there was an inner place where I didn't trust myself with anything.

As I was leaving that wine bar, a man, probably in his seventies, entered the place with the cutest little dog, which I, being a chronic stalker of other people's pets, immediately fussed over. He spoke no English, I an increasing but still inadequate amount of Italian. One thing I was learning about language: it also helped make clear people's unstated intentions. I had never considered that aspect of it before this trip.

He told me his name was Norman, I think, or maybe he said he was a Norman. He was German born but proudly Italian, proudly Veronese in particular. He said his dog was a biter, so be careful. Not much later, as I left the bar, I found him waiting for me outside. Speaking a constant stream, he led me across the street and showed me inside the Chiesa San Giovanni in Foro, which truly was worthy of showing off, twelfth century with Roman archaeological remains inside. Then we went around the corner to another church and another bar, where he bought me a drink that I did not drink, but the bar was a beauty, the Caffè Monte Baldo, an old, atmospheric side-street find.

We established he was a retired labourer on the pension who was appalled that Australians generally didn't have a second language (he was right, it is appalling) and that Pino, his dog, did not bite at all, my mistake, but was keenly into bar snacks.

I got edgy and uncomfortable and attempted to tell him I needed to go home, while still trying to be polite. He asked where I lived and I told him and then we were heading that way. An hour after we had left the bar, this sweet, simple, nice but not-my-kind-of-person man and I reached the front door. I was apprehensive of his expectations but he seemed to have none. Or if he did, he didn't voice them. Or I didn't understand them. We said goodbye, he asked if I wanted to go and have more *apertivo* instead. I said no, thank you, good night again. And closed the door.

And then I caught a glimpse of Norman and Pino wandering off and I felt like crying. This was the moment in which I felt I had disappointed. Rejecting people broke my heart to pieces. It was why I had agreed to too much sex on first dates (not that this was ever on the cards with Norman), too many one-night stands, and let too many people into my life that I really shouldn't have. I guess it was what some less honourable people saw in me. It devastated me to say no and they sensed it. That whole fear-of-being-disliked thing again, the people pleaser, the play-nice girl.

And so I got mad at God. In fact, I did a bit of yelling in his direction. Out loud. 'Your sense of humour is not only inappropriate right now, but also not appreciated. I do not understand why the only males I attract are gay guys, small children and old men. I figure it's because you think it's funny.' I stomped to the bedroom, threw off my shoes, and stopped at the mirror. 'If this is not you being funny, is this the problem? That I have tickets on myself? That I think myself hotter, smarter, funnier, generally better than I am? Because that is a serious problem. Are you adjusting my expectations and showing me the best I can feasibly anticipate? This sucks, God. I really don't get why this is what you have chosen for me. I DO NOT GET IT. So best you explain it.'

I swear I heard giggling. Not much else.

Why couldn't I simply enjoy the opportunity for a nice walk with a nice old guy? Why did I turn it into *War and Peace*? Somewhere along the way I had lost the capability to enjoy life. I actually wondered if I ever had it. The Italians seemed to have it in buckets.

I had intensely vivid memories of things falling from the sky, a Chinese satellite, Skylab. During some key fire-ups of the Cold War, I thought the world was going to end. On 9/11, I was sure it was all over. I'd been expecting Armageddon for as long as I could remember. I wondered about the more sensitive or neurotic among us, baby boomers and Gen Xers who were constantly subject to this stuff: how many of us trusted at all and could let go and enjoy? We had been raised on fear, and unrealised fear at that. No matter how nurturing and stable our homes, we were surrounded by fear.

In Verona, the Nazis came to the doorstep and bombed bridges. The Veronese rebuilt those bridges and life went on. In Australia, the generations of my parents and their parents went to war, confronted the enemy, and life went on.

We sat around and waited for the worst, a cataclysmic showdown of superpowers that never happened. Thank God. But you know, the Cold War had ended. I was still worrying. I was so over it. It was time to enjoy life. It surely was.

14

Ravenna

'Tis vain to struggle, I have struggled long
To love again no more as I once loved.
Oh! Time! Why leave this earliest passion strong?
To tear a heart which pants to be unmoved?

To the Po. June 2nd 1819

They had each other at *buongiorno*. Lord Byron met the young *contessa*, Teresa Guiccioli, at a party in Venice. The very next day, while her husband napped, Teresa was sneaking off to engage desires with the poet, an act that would be on regular repeat for the next four years. It is said that Teresa was his most enduring, possibly most meaningful love. Save for Augusta, which, of course, was forbidden love of the most forbidden kind.

Mind you, the love between Lord Byron and Teresa was not conventional and not without its difficulties and danger either. From letters between the two it's clear that it was a push–pull relationship full of high drama, tears, big gestures and tempestuous make-up sex. By today's standards, they were hardly your pin-up couple for healthy love. By Italian nobility standards of the 1800s, the only thing that was out of the ordinary was Teresa's occasional indiscretion about the affair. While adulteries were accepted as a way of life and blind eyes were turned, society's unwritten law was that the lovers at least appear to keep it on the down-low. Teresa was not particularly good at that.

But she was nineteen, Lord Byron thirty. Teresa's husband, Count Alessandro Guiccioli, was somewhere over fifty. The two men had sophistication she did not—though she was no piece of fluff. She came from a good family and was highly intelligent, inquisitive and educated.

The count had a pedigree and past that gave Byron's a run for its lira. Immensely wealthy in land holdings, if not cash, and with influence that ran all the way to the Vatican and the cunning and ruthlessness one needed for that, Count Guiccioli, like many an Italian nobleman before him and no doubt after him, had been involved in assassinations and, rumour had it, disposed of wife number one with a well-placed dose of poison.

Dangerous liaisons indeed, and Byron thrived on those. But his attraction to Teresa was not entirely the result of his usual compulsions and motivations. She was smart and funny and he felt at ease with her.

They had only ten days of tryst in Venice before the Guicciolis travelled back to their home in Ravenna, a seaside town about 140 kilometres of road south in the province of Emilia Romagna. Receiving word that Teresa had fallen ill on the way, Lord Byron followed. Ravenna was well and truly off the tourist map. Though it had been the seat of the Roman Empire and all manner of other important things, it was 'out of the way of travellers and armies', as Lord Byron put it in a letter to Lady Byron, and so had a freshness and purity to it that delighted him. He would not settle there till the following year, though. For months, the Guicciolis and Lord Byron were on the move, in a bizarre dance of power, passion and jealousy. It began when the count could no longer bear the prattle of the affair in the streets of Ravenna, and moved Teresa to their property in Bologna. Lord Byron followed. The count put up with it for a while then moved Teresa again, this time on a tour of their properties throughout the region.

Byron stayed in Bologna. For reasons that Byron's friends hypothesised were likely clandestine, calculated and very probably fiscal, the count then returned to Bologna with his wife, before taking off on his own for Ravenna, leaving the lovers to make their own way to Venice together, where Lord Byron still had Mocenigo leased and where the frail-of-health Teresa could see her physician.

The trip, a jaunt through the country taking in Padua, Arquà Petrarca and Mira, had all the qualities of a honeymoon, and it cemented them together.

What gave a right place, right time inevitability to Lord Byron and Teresa Guiccioli's union was that he was over the hurdy-gurdy of sex he'd been on. In some ways, as when he'd met Annabella, he was in a phase. 'I am in love, and tired of promiscuous concubinage, and have now an opportunity of settling for life,' he wrote to his friend Hobhouse a month after meeting the *contessa*. And in his ode addressed to the River Po, which flows to Ravenna, written to Teresa while he was travelling it, he reveals that he had sworn off love altogether prior to her coming into his life.

It's a universal truth that when you stop looking for love it finds you. An equally strong truth is that when you are absolutely resolute in what you want and what you don't want, love appears. For Lord Byron at least, both cosmic rules came into play at once. They seem simple laws. But like Lord Byron had to, sometimes we need to push ourselves through life's sieve to refine our desires. It is as painful as it sounds.

*

I went to Ravenna on that first trip to Italy after the magazine debacle. I read in the Lonely Planet guide that it had very cool fourth- and fifth-century mosaics. I had no interest whatsoever in mosaics, but the guide also said it was off the beaten track and that intrigued me. It was the first month of spring then, and I drove north from Florence to Bologna, then peeled off to the east, passing through flat plains of fruit trees beginning to blossom and fields fallow yet potent in their promise of summer's burgeoning.

Now, as I approached Ravenna in June and by train, those fields were neck deep in vibrant crops and the trees dripped with sumptuous foliage and juicy fruit. And then came the outskirts. Ravenna, like so many Italian towns, is ringed with ugly industry, Ravenna more so than most because of its proximity to the Adriatic and the gateway to oilfields and to the east that provides.

The railway station is modern and the buildings that greet you as you leave it lack charm, to be kind about it. The city bears the scars of World War II and the fifties and sixties' craze for modernisation that swept parts of Italy. The main thoroughfare from the station to the *centro storico*, is a busy bus terminus. It's a catwalk lined with not only Italian men, who've no doubt sat along that street for decades, but also groups of African migrants and gangs of youths who take up what bench space there is left and don't mind one little bit if you are intimidated. Across the street a large, open car park and an ugly modern hotel exterior do not do much more for first impressions.

But a mere block behind all that is the first inkling of Ravenna's true heart. Look past those groups of men sitting watching you, and you will see that they have their backs to San Giovanni Evangelista, a church dating back to the year

420 when it was built by a Roman princess, Galla Placidia, as a thank you to Saint John the Evangelist whom she believed had listened to her prayers from a boat in the middle of a tempest and delivered her safely to the Adriatic shore. Done up by twelfth-century monks, damaged during and restored after the war, the church is nonetheless a bastion of this city's real character and depth of meaning.

Ravenna, now home to 140 000 people, was at various times the capital of the Western Roman Empire; the hub of the reign of Teodorico, King of the Goths; and the seat of the Empire of Byzantium in Europe. You expect that kind of back-story in places that remain capitals. What's amazing about Ravenna is that it's now not exactly a backwater, but certainly not one of Italy's star cities. Yet it played a vital role in a succession of different civilisations.

On my first trip to Ravenna, I had arrived with no bookings. The centre of town is a car-free zone, other than for pick-ups, drop-offs, deliveries and taxis. I had left my car in the railway lot and wandered, asking at several ugly hotels for a room, to no avail. The first one I found a vacancy at had been the Hotel Centrale Byron, right in the middle of the historic area but reflective more of the city's modernisation than its history. Especially of its history with Byron. So I was delighted, on this, my second visit, that my punt on booking from home (sight unseen) a B&B called A Casa di Paola paid off immediately. It was on an interesting cobbled street lined with *palazzi*, some even dating back to the fifteenth century, and was itself a nineteenth-century mansion with a big wooden door right on the street.

Paola, a former model, had a thing for Chinese antiques and a good eye for décor, evident in the airy main foyer out through which she led me to the back garden where my little stand-alone cottage was. The garden, which adjoined the fifth-century Battistero degli Ariani, or Arian Baptistry, one of Ravenna's most important ancient religious sites, was shady and somewhat disorderly, full of pots and palms, bamboo and a large pine entwined in ivy.

My cottage had a small kitchen with a table, a big bedroom and a terracotta-tiled bathroom. Best of all, right outside were a wooden table and chairs shaded by the pine tree. Not so great, however, was the very loud clock tower tolling every fifteen minutes somewhere nearby. I soon discovered it was the clock in the main square, right out the back of my cottage, and it would sound solemnly every fifteen minutes every day from seven in the morning till 1 a.m. You do get used to these things, but 1 a.m.!

I also quickly discovered I was living right near the central market. I bought tomatoes, ham, olives, pecorino, basil, peaches, apricots and nectarines, lettuce and a crunchy brown bread the Italians call *integrale*.

In the cool of the evening I sat down at my outside table with my repast, and recommenced reading Fiona McCarthy's book on Lord Byron. She noted that he arrived there on 10 June, which coincidently was this day, the day I had arrived too.

'*Ciao! Ciao!* (insert lots of Italian here)' An attractive, vivacious woman of a senior age with blonde curls, and an excellent figure shown off in floral three-quarter pants and a plunging pink shirt, came waving and gesticulating out of another apartment diagonally across the garden from me.

'*Mi dispiace, signora, non parlo Italiano!*' I called out as she approached, all smiles and radiance and welcome and incomprehensibility.

'*No? Oh, come si chiama?*'

I knew this one. '*Mi chiamo Julietta.*'

'*Ciao, Julietta!*' She kissed me and hugged me with the warmth and familiarity of a favourite dressing gown, telling me her name was Luciana, Paola's mother. She had two dogs, Alice (Al-ee-chay), a way-too-fat beagle, and a shih tzu whose name I never did catch despite asking several people about a dozen times what it was. That shih tzu came up to you with all the charm in the world, lured you in for the pat then, when you were feeling you and he were firm friends, he turned around and gave you a solid nip if you were not quick enough to pull your hand away. I loved him for his fickleness, like Lord Byron loved his tempestuous Italian mistresses. Such a challenge.

The thing I had discovered about Italians is that many don't believe you when you say you don't speak their language, or you can't understand it, especially when you say a few phrases, and quite well; I put a lot of swagger into my Italian accent, all sing-song and rolled Rs when I got the opportunity to exercise it, so I had no one else to blame but myself.

But more times than I could count, at railway station ticket booths, cafés and kiosks, my '*Non parlo Italiano*' had been met with the response, '*Si, si parla Italiano.*' Yes, you speak Italian. I had just spoken Italian, therefore I spoke Italian: another wonderful example of Italy's unique logic.

Luciana fell into the disbeliever category. In a rush of her native language, she introduced me to her dogs, appeared to tell me a number of things about the house, garden, neighbourhood, weather, time of day and season, her outfit and I think her hair, then said something about '*mangiato*'.

'*No, grazie,*' I said, believing she had asked me if I wanted something to eat. I had already eaten; the remnants of the antipasti dinner I had prepared for myself were still on the table.

'*Benissimo,*' she exclaimed and bustled back to her place.

The duplicitous shih tzu stayed, intent on getting some of the leftover prosciutto from my table, which he did, then gave me a quick nip by way of thanks.

Luciana returned with two plates of poached eggs, some dried biscuits and a bottle of chianti. Clearly I hadn't quite made my position obvious on the whole eating thing. She must have asked me if I had eaten, rather than if I was hungry.

Getting a bike in a town that ran on pedal power was like visiting a hospital in other places. Ravenna was a big cycling town. Flat and car free, it was made for it. Former Giro d'Italia winner Luciano Sambi had a bike shop outside the gates of old Ravenna and it was busy and earnest. There were a million things going on all at once, all seemingly critically important. There was the elderly lady picking up the bicycle that looked as if it had been her essential mode of transport for at least the past two decades. Rust and all, she and it were treated as seriously as the young fit enthusiast with the fancy new wheels. There was a man at the counter choosing a pump. He was shown four, which were discussed at length in the context of his needs and liabilities. There were sick bikes lined up for attention and a sea of them waiting to be picked up.

I was hiring a bike for my stay and Signor Sambi himself was fixing up what was to be my transport. On the wall there were clipped newspaper articles about him as a younger man winning that Giro. I figured I was in good hands. Soon I had two wheels again and it felt excellent—although this was my first wheel-on-cobblestones experience, so it had its discomfort, that's for sure.

I rode my steed ten kilometres to the beach, along a bike path that ran through fields practically all the way. The old town had ritzy shops, lovely restaurants, cobbled streets and those great old monuments. But outside were high rises and heavy petrochemical industry. The province of Emilia Romagna has a generally high standard of living. But it gets it from being busy and obviously the coastline of the Adriatic is not just for pleasure. There is fuel out there. I could see the platforms from the shore.

The bike path didn't go near all the industry though. I saw the factories, plants and smoke stacks on the horizon as I passed through wheat and cornfields and orchards.

The Adriatic at the Ravennese seashore was a bowl of cold soup, a flat, unchanging mass, quite like Port Phillip Bay, whose shore hosted our family beach sojourns in the 1960s and seventies. Dad led those expeditions on his irregular times home with the family at Lavender Street. He would submit the lot of us to his restlessness and we'd pile into the Holden station wagon for the long trip from Ringwood, at the foot of the Dandenong Ranges, to the beach at Seaford. Now there were freeways and even the most basic cars had air-conditioning. Plus, there were laws against having that many people in a car. But it was all of us together and off we'd go, Esky full and spirits up. I remember hot sand underfoot and setting up camp in the tea-tree forest in the dunes, crickets chirping, us kids drinking cordial out of coloured aluminium cups. You couldn't set up camp in those dunes today, let alone drive in and create your own little shady hollow with the help of a tomahawk before setting up your tarp, tables, chairs and little camp fire for the billy of tea like Dad used to. It's all protected now.

Likewise the vegetation that lay between the simple beach houses at the Ravenna seaside and the actual sand. It was protected, too. There were shady streets of pleasantly faded dwellings. Then there was a sliver of the forest of pines and ivy through which Lord Byron had liked to ride his horse. Beyond that there was the beach lined with the *bagni*: bars and cafés that rented out beach chairs and umbrellas.

The whole effect was casual and a bit scruffy, not rundown or unpleasant. It was laid back and old-school beachy, in a worker's holiday way. This was not the Riviera. And it was entirely comfortable for someone like me who detests the idea of the beach as catwalk.

I had my lounge and umbrella, seven euro for a half day. On the sand in front of me and on the loungers in rows surrounding there were kids with buckets, looked after by old ladies the colour and texture of a deflated Aussie Rules football. Old men lay on their backs, bellies up in the air like the Sydney Harbour Bridge. There were sailing boats bobbing beyond man-made breaks and people playing table soccer and ping-pong. No one was swimming, though some were wading. Swings and a plastic jungle gym provided entertainment for some little ones.

African touts harassed beachgoers with Louis Vuitton and Gucci knock-off belts, boards of jewellery, hats, bandannas, trinkets, toy monkeys, Alice bands with devil horns attached and novelty rubber balls.

There were families everywhere. Again, I was the only one alone. I began to get fidgety.

I did not believe the *he* I seemed to be perpetually seeking still was going to find me sitting in the corner of the garden at Casa di Paola or lying on a banana lounge reading a book about Lord Byron surrounded by couples and children at the beach. Why was *he* so important? I did know that I was doing my best at all of this. And maybe that was the problem. That I was trying to *do* life instead of live it. Trying to get it right instead of just getting it.

And then, if I was honest, alcohol and I were not mixing well. I did know that I had felt very lonely these past few days since I'd got to Ravenna, especially at the beach. And I knew that

I had been going to bars in the evening, allegedly to do as the locals did, to soak up the atmosphere. But I was undoubtedly looking for him. I could completely see why I was drinking and it was not for the pleasure of it. It was loaded with emotional back-story—and it was another version of the old story, whatever that was. I was out looking for him and, in Ravenna, that pretty much meant sitting with a glass of wine. It had great little bars and a lively *apertivo* culture. The Italians doing it so well again. But I was struggling to make it work for me.

It wasn't the drink itself. I had a chasmic love void, a devastating loneliness that had risen up to meet me since the strange episodes of Claudio and Norman. Until that was reconciled I could not move forward. He was not in a bar. He was not in a bottle. I knew this. And neither was my salvation. I needed to stop looking.

Lying on the beach there, I made my decision. The search was over. Truly, deeply, I was ready to accept myself as a single woman, I told myself. I had to be. Otherwise I was going to end up in that pit of despair again.

In the evening, I headed out for dinner, cycling the streets, looking for somewhere that appealed. I ventured down a quiet laneway and walked into a trattoria at which I had yet to eat. The *signora* was in the process of seating me at a table and telling me I had to be out of the tiny establishment at nine to make way for a booking when a man walked in solo. In dreadful Italian he asked for a table and she seated him at one a metre or so from me and told him he had to vacate at half past eight. There was no one else in there. We both studied the Italian-language-only menu and it felt a bit awkward, the two of us being English speakers. The waitress came to me, I asked what a dish on the menu was, found out it was rabbit, she told me the specials and I ordered the meatballs with peas, a salad and a bottle of aqua naturale, *per favore*.

After she left for the kitchen with my order, he looked over. 'Did you catch any of that?' he said.

'All I caught was rabbit and meatballs.'

He pulled out a big Italian dictionary. 'I'm trying to learn Italian while I'm here.' When the waitress came back to the dining room, of course she spoke to him in English. He ordered in Italian.

'Bravo,' I said, after she had gone to the kitchen with his order. I went back to my notebook.

'Where are you from?' he called over, as more people began arriving at the restaurant. I told him, and went on to what I was doing in Ravenna.

'And you?'

'From Nottinghamshire,' he said.

'Where Lord Byron's house is!'

'Yes, but it's not really a house, more a pile of stone and a park now,' he said of Newstead Abbey, the Byron ancestral home.

More people had arrived; we were forced to yell to be heard by each other, and duck this way and that to keep each other in eye line as other diners passed by.

'Would you like to join me at this table?' I asked when it was becoming absurd.

'Yes, thank you.'

His name was Paul. He was unmannered but not awkward, seemingly unselfconscious but easy to blush. Smart and witty. He had a great smile, great teeth. Funny what we notice. He was well read and had recently finished a book about Greek history that gave him a strong perspective on Lord Byron. 'He was a bit of a plonker, really. The Greeks took him to the cleaners while he walked around in the little uniforms he had made for himself. But if he hadn't died in Greece, the English never would have got involved and liberation wouldn't have happened when it did. So in the end, he did achieve his aim.'

Extremely well travelled, another adventurer, he had lived a few years here and there. He worked in the petrochemical business, which is what had recently brought him to Ravenna. We compared notes on places we had been. I mentioned that after Ravenna I was going next to Pisa and how non-Italians I mentioned this to had told me how much they didn't like the Tuscan town.

'I think Pisa's lovely,' Paul said. 'A great city.'

I told him of the trattoria I had discovered the day before but couldn't remember the street and didn't have the card with me. I offered him mine and suggested he email me if he wanted to and I would furnish him with the details. 'Or,' I said, 'perhaps we can dine there together some time. If you feel like company, SMS me or something.' He rummaged for his card, but didn't have one, so wrote his email address and phone number on a piece of paper.

Nine o'clock came and we parted. As I rode back to Paola's I reflected on how I had checked for a wedding ring before I gave him my card. The check was a reflex, but the invitation was extended without expectation, hooks or even hope. I was no longer looking in that moment. But I knew I would like to see him again.

15

Bagnacavallo

What deep wounds ever closed without a scar?
The heart's bleed longest, and but heal to wear
That which disfigures it; and they who war
With their own hopes, and have been vanquish'd bear
Silence, but not submission: in his lair
Fix'd Passion holds his breath, until the hour
Which shall atone for years; none need despair:
It came, it cometh, and will come,—the power
To punish or forgive—in one, we shall be slower.

Childe Harold's Pilgrimage, Canto III

While Lord Byron and Teresa were in the throes of intense new obsession, traipsing about the Veneto and Emilia Romagna, Allegra, still in Venice and in her third year on earth, was billeted with a series of caretakers; first, the British Consul General Richard Hoppner and his wife. The Hoppners didn't much like her, citing bed-wetting, sullenness and developmental slowness as their reasons. They palmed her off onto the family of one of their servants, then to the family of the Danish Consul. Lord Byron eventually sent for her to be brought to him in Bologna.

He then took her, along with his menagerie, to Ravenna, where he leased from the husband of his lover the top floor of the Palazzo Guiccioli, thus putting the child in a curious position. Though she may not have witnessed the sexual secrets, intrigue and power plays, she would have been living in the tense atmosphere the arrangement between Lord Byron and the Guicciolis must have created. Children are little sponges. They may not understand the tension in the air, but they feel it. The adults with whom she resided were not the most stable of human beings. Teresa wavered between spoiling Allegra and resenting her. Claire Clairmont, the child's mother, was notably absent, Lord Byron refusing to have her in his vicinity.

By the time Allegra was four, Lord Byron and Teresa were embroiled in revolutionary politics. Her father was preoccupied not only with that and the writing of *Don Juan*, but also with the vitriolic backlash against him in England. He made a decision to send the child away to a convent, San Giovanni Batista, in a small town called Bagnacavallo. A year later, Allegra died there, of what is generally agreed to have been typhus, having never seen her father again.

Do men of great individuality always make bad fathers? Which is not to ask whether all great fathers are men who lack individuality. But I suspect there is a level of selflessness required for excellent parenting that neither Lord Byron nor my father had.

Some people find it impossible to put aside their own stuff to become good parents. I occasionally wonder what kind of a mother I might have made, with my wandering ways and love of the alone. I do love both those things, but I also adore kids, family and, of course, love itself. Maybe being a parent would have made me a better person. Maybe not. It seems a pointless hypothetical.

I thought of Lord Byron's decision to have poor little Allegra packed off to the nuns after having lived in a *palazzo* with poets. Like me, she probably believed she was responsible for everything; she surely must have believed she had done something frightfully wrong to be banished like that.

Riding a bike in Ravenna could be, at times, not unlike driving in Florence. I was going to say driving in Rome but I have never done that. I have driven in Florence, however, and I have the traffic citation to prove it. At least with the cars in Florence there is some small semblance of traffic laws. On busy days, like Tuesdays apparently, Ravenna is one big game of two-wheeled chicken, with obstinate or oblivious pedestrians thrown in to make competition all the more interesting.

In one morning alone I had more almost-prangs with speeding *nonnas* than anyone should have in a lifetime. Some of those *nonnas* had not one, but two *bambini* on board, one in the front handlebars baby seat, another on the seat up the back. There were many delivery vans in town, too. It was dodgem city: people riding the wrong side of the street; pedestrians and other cyclists stopped for a chat in the middle of a tiny cobbled lane, with everyone forced to go around and some refusing to slow or even back down at the threat of a head-on. Everyone was vying for that little strip of smoother, but still bumpy, white cobbles down the middle of the street, which was also where you encountered Hummer-sized prams.

It was exhilarating.

I had yet to find my gelateria in Ravenna, though. That was not exhilarating. It was very frustrating. The Ravennese gelaterias were okay, but none of them lived up to Ponte Pietra in Verona. Perhaps nothing ever would. But I had found a great café at the base of an ugly orange-brick six-storey apartment block in a back street not far from Paola's. It was called Fargo and the pastries were organic, the coffee was wicked and the hipsters and *nonnas* in the know went there. It had taken over a tiny square with cane chairs and cute iron tables. Every morning I was having a *crema*, a custard-filled *cornetto*, this particular version being spectacularly well balanced between sweet and creamy (the custard), flaky and chewy (the pastry). I washed it down with two *caffè lunghi*. How was it that it was perfectly acceptable to me to have custard-filled pastry for breakfast in Europe, but in Australia I'd consider it a travesty of blood sugar level fluctuations, refined flour intolerances and nutrition-negative kilojoules?

Paul told me he had seen, near his apartment, a plaque that commemorated a spot where Byron had slept. Every day I doffed my lid at the Palazzo Guiccioli on Via Cavour—what was, these days, Ravenna's main shopping street—but I had yet to find this other place. The morning after we shared that meal, as I got off my bike at Fargo, I received a text message from him giving me exact instructions as to the plaque's whereabouts. I texted back a thank you and a quick note about my day.

I did not hear back.

Each year, Ravenna has a summer arts festival that has featured some of the greatest orchestras in the world, and Bob Dylan. My visit to the town coincided with the festival and so I booked some tickets. I had no idea what to expect of my first event, because most of the available promotional material was in Italian. I knew it was a piano recital and it started at half-past nine in the evening, which seemed so late to me until I turned up and discovered it was outside on the treed lawn of the porticoed courtyard in the centre of the Biblioteca Classense. The Classense is where Lord Byron's letters to Teresa are held in safekeeping.

As it turned out, the concert was a plink-plonk repertoire of modern composers who refused to believe there are only so many ways to peel an orange. People walked out. Others, like myself, stayed till the end when the best bits occurred, the playing with the elbows, the flat palms and the fists. And then the messing about on the Steinway's strings, with no regard for the keys, the pianists' head under the hood like a car mechanic.

I knew there was a place for this stuff, like in horror movies for example. And I got that it was wonderfully well played.

'Did you enjoy it?' the elegant Ravennese society *signora* seated next to me asked.

'It was interesting,' I answered, which was the truth.

I did try to beat my prejudice of wanting a little melody and rhythm in my piano recitals. (Call me old-fashioned, but I do.) So I wiggled my shoulders a bit to relax them, took a few deep breaths and closed my eyes to see what might be evoked by that music: the moments of absurdity pushed up against anger and doom, suddenly opening to windows of something like harmony and rhythm but only for a short time and then more melody but not entirely right, big bursts of frenetic sounds followed by sparse melancholy.

All I could think of was my last relationship. Discord, unpredictability, disharmony. The thing that reminded me most of that relationship was the excruciating ache, during the cacophony, for the melodious brackets. And then when they came, that terrible make-do pretence that near enough was good enough.

I woke up 'lemancholy' the next day, as Lord Byron called his melancholy. I didn't think the plink-plonk was to blame. It was my soul, as usual, two steps ahead of me, knowing that

I was going to Bagnacavallo, the place where little Allegra Byron died at five years of age.

I decided to take my bike on the train to Bagnacavallo, less than twenty kilometres inland from Ravenna. But it was a bit of a to-do. The train was already in the station, twenty minutes before it was due to depart. I got on an empty carriage in the middle. A guard came and, in Italian, told me I could not have my bike there. 'Last carriage,' he said in English. So I hauled my bike off and headed to the end of the train, where I got on the last, also empty carriage. Ten minutes later the guard found me again. 'No. Not first carriage, last carriage,' he said in English, waggling his finger. He watched me haul my bike off again, flustered, red-faced, then he walked in front of me all the way up to the engine.

'Isn't this the first carriage?'

He didn't respond, but watched me lug my bike onto the train again, into another empty carriage, where there was a section full of bike rails. Not on the ground, though. You had to lift your bike and hang the front wheel off some hooks that were way above my head. He motioned to the hooks and watched me struggle for several minutes trying to get my bike, the only bike on the train, onto one of these hooks, which, I discovered, were not only above my head, but several centimetres above my fully extended reach. I got my bike into place. He left me with a self-satisfied nodding of his head. The train departed the station, with my bike and me the sole occupants of that carriage. Five minutes later he was back, checking my ticket, validated, and then my bike ticket, which was not validated. I didn't realise you had to do both. I've never seen a human being more pleased to be in a position of authority. I teared up. With a great, sudden flourish of benevolence, he let me off but could not resist a waggle-fingered warning. I'd made his day.

Bagnacavallo is an absurdly picturesque little town, so authentic as to practically be corny: narrow winding streets built on a medieval corkscrew with peeling walls and quiet *piazze* of antique appeal and symmetry. I arrived just as that quietness which descends on Italian villages at lunchtime blanketed each and every corner of the place. It did not take long for my bike and me to find the exact location where Allegra had died. It felt desolate. A nice, although unremarkable church fronted a small, rectangular courtyard with a row of egg-shaped topiaries for a fence; a firmly shut door, in that way some doors are more shut than others, leading to the Capuchin cloister. There was a plaque above the door that said more about Allegra's papa being Lord Byron and the fact that Shelley had visited than her death.

I felt her loneliness. I felt that she had been misjudged. In all the reading I'd done, Allegra had been accused of all sorts of surliness, of having been brattish and greedy, selfish and needy. At one point before Lord Byron left Ravenna for Pisa, crossing the country, leaving her in the east while he went west, which was across a narrow part of the country but may as well have been to the moon, he received a letter from Allegra, begging him to visit—and asking him to bring toys. He focused on the asking for toys. That was the real motivation for her wanting to see him, he said, not to be with her father. So he did not visit.

I was eighteen and in my university days. I had a job to pay for a lot of my expenses. Though my mum had, in my final year at school, won that Lotto money, she still had to work. It was not a big sum and after she'd paid all her debts it was a good deal smaller. As I became increasingly miserable in that first year of university, Mum put me into a boarding facility on campus where I had a couple of friends, in the hope that it would make life easier on me. It was an expensive exercise. She was a generous woman who had enormous faith in me.

But she also decided to take my father back to court to hit him up for some help with the university expenses. I think now that it was her final opportunity to have a really good go at him; she could have told me to get on with it, after all. She was, as I said, a generous woman who loved me to bits, especially as I got older and displayed the same interests as her, in literature and language. But some scars are deep.

Those on Mum's side of the family fence—me, Bernadette, a brother or two—turned up at Melbourne's family court to demand maintenance from the old man, as we called him.

There he was, the old man—and his lawyer. He had good lawyers because he dealt a lot with the murky side of things in his journalistic work. We had legal aid, but as it turned out, the woman we were given was a highly talented litigator who went on to be head of the Supreme Court or some such. Which is neither here nor there, except that things got ugly in that courtroom.

Witnesses were left to wait in anterooms. There was lots of laughter from us when, in this Melbourne government building of the early eighties, I discovered the partitioning between courtroom and anteroom did not go all the way to the window of the high rise. If you put your ear to the gap, you could hear what was going on.

Our way was to make fun of the big stuff, treat life's trials as a bit of hilarious sport. Here we were, doing it again and, clever me, I'd found a way to get one up on the old man: listen in when we weren't supposed to.

And so we listened. The big important moments for me were these: overhearing my mum being quizzed about the food allergies I had which she had listed as part of the expense of keeping me; the fact that I had worked in milk bars, etc., since I was fourteen seeming to be an excuse for my father to not contribute to my upbringing; my clothing allowances and other expenses being questioned; and there was something about my need for a university degree. I wanted to be a journalist. My father had become a journalist without one, lots of others had, why did I need one? And then that moment, from Dad's lawyer, 'I put it to you, your honour, that Miss Jameson is one very spoiled young lady.'

After my mother left the dock it was my turn. I stepped up onto that podium and sat down on that seat, and my father's lawyer began on me, about me being a bad daughter because I did not try to have contact with him. 'He didn't have contact with us!' I said. And I broke down uncontrollably. I see now that all the years of feeling poor, of hiding when the police and the debt collectors came because he hadn't paid bills or fines, all the grief from years of knowing his chronic lack of willingness to pay maintenance, the sheer fact of his abandonment, my still then very active denial that I had been in any way affected by my parents' divorce, all this swamped me. Dad's lawyer kept going and I couldn't speak for gasping, heaving, wailing.

I recall our lawyer asking for a stay for me to get myself together, and the judge letting me go, saying there was no need for me to come back. She'd made up her mind.

And of course, in the anteroom, I was a hero. My 'performance' was brilliant. Yes, wasn't it, I agreed. What an actress, me, just like my mother. The judge needed no more evidence. The old man had proven himself to be a cheap scoundrel. He had to pay. Which of course, he never did, but I suspect that was not what we were there for.

And one more pertinent memory: as we were leaving the court, the old man popped over to our camp and suggested we all go for a beer—as if we'd just played a game of footy and he was someone who used to play for our team but now played for the opposition.

We didn't go.

Lord Byron wrote congenially to his estranged wife, Lady Byron, till his death. That strange dissociation with unpleasantness, there's a lot of what we these days call narcissist disorder in that. My dad had an extraordinary talent for it that his children would come up against time and time again. Life was a series of games from which he wouldn't back down till he won. He'd expect everyone to shake hands and be good sports about it. Go for a beer. Even the court case: he probably thought he'd won because he knew he was never going to pay up anyway, and had gone through the motions knowing my mother wouldn't have the energy, or the heart, to take him back to court again.

He did some terrible things to my brothers and sisters, of the mentally and emotionally tormenting kind—he was not a violent man, but he was a mind-fucker. He just loved to be. We could all trot out a yarn about how he did that, about our own personal episodes.

Allegra Byron and I shared more than just 12 January as our birthday. We shared terrible fathers, and we shared parents who used us as currency in their war against each other. At least I was being given the opportunity to bring my sadness up for examination. Allegra didn't live long enough to even be aware of hers in any meaningful sense, other than becoming fractious because of it, then dying, I thought, of abandonment and loneliness. Though I didn't know I had made much more progress than Allegra. As a woman in her forties, only just becoming aware of how much she had pushed the pain of all this down, it was clear that a great part of me had been walking dead for far too many years. The part of me that wanted to believe trustworthy, respectful love was not only possible but my right and due, this is what had been dormant.

What would it take to have me believe in that again? Would it take that kind of love actually turning up? Or could it not turn up until I believed? By asking the question, I could feel the stirrings of a sense of worthiness attempting to come out from under its blanket of early experience. And it didn't feel bad at all.

16

Piazza del Popolo

Oh, Love! What is it in this world of ours
Which makes it fatal to be loved? Ah why
With cypress branches hast thou wreathed thy bowers,
And made thy best interpreter a sigh?

Don Juan, Canto III

'Lord Byron gets up at *two*.' That was p.m., according to Percy Shelley, who wrote of visiting his friend in Ravenna:

'From six to eight we gallop through the pine forests which divide Ravenna from the sea; we then come home and dine, and sit up gossiping till six in the morning ... Lord B.'s establishment consists, besides servants, of ten horses, eight enormous dogs, three monkeys, five cats, an eagle, a crow, and a falcon; and all these, except the horses, walk about the house, which every now and then resounds with their unarbitrated quarrels, as if they were the masters of it ... (P.S.) I find that my enumeration of the animals in this Circean Palace was defective ... I have just met on the grand staircase five peacocks, two guinea hens, and an Egyptian crane.'

*

Lord Byron was enjoying life in Ravenna, particularly riding in those glorious pine forests, and the mix of rusticity and sophistication the town had then.

But trouble was brewing.

The early cantos of *Don Juan* had been savaged in London as 'filthy and impious' work from 'an unrepenting, unsoftened, smiling, sarcastic, joyous sinner'. Lord Byron was unable to brush it off but he stood firm: this was his best writing yet, he believed. While his publisher John Murray pleaded with him to clean up the cantos, Lord Byron would not budge. Teresa was not a fan of the work, either.

Things in the poet's life were building to their crescendo. Though Alessandro Guiccioli had to have known about the affair—he had a network of spies and snitches throughout the *palazzo*, as Lord Byron and Teresa had also—it was when he broke into Teresa's writing desk and found the correspondence between the lovers that tensions reached untenable heights. Teresa's father, Count Gamba, stepped in, using his own papal connections to secure a decree releasing Teresa from her marriage.

Ravenna then was a papal state and paranoia about civil unrest was setting in. The loose-cannon poet was beginning to be seen as a threat. A subversive underground, the Carbonari, was gaining strength throughout Italy, intent on rising up against Austrian rule. At first unbeknown to Lord Byron, Teresa's family, the Gambas, were heavily involved in the Carbonari. When he did find out, it was not long before he too became embroiled.

And it would not be long before the Gambas would be banished from Ravenna because of their links, forcing Lord Byron to leave the city too. 'It is an awful work, this love, and prevents all a man's projected of good or glory. I wanted to go to Greece lately (as everything seems up here),' he wrote to Thomas Moore. 'But the tears of a woman who has left her husband for a man, and the weakness of one's own heart, are paramount to these projects, and I can hardly indulge them.'

No man is an island, not even one as enduringly singular in his pursuit of self-interest as Lord Byron. Our relationships impact upon us fundamentally. Our choice of associates can seem to take us in directions we never intended. But we know. At the outset we know. Intuition tells us. The uh-oh, or the ah-ha. For a split second, we are conscious of it. It tells us all we need to know. We choose whether to ignore that knowledge or heed it. Lord Byron knew, perhaps even on a soul level before he met Teresa, that in making a decision to link his destiny to hers, life was going to move in a profoundly different direction. On that deep level he must have wanted that. He committed fully to going with it.

Our choice of relationships and the paths they take us down can have astonishing consequences, revealing aspects of ourselves of which we had no previous idea. Those choices are quite possibly the best choices. They may not deliver the expected outcomes. But like Lord Byron's choice of Teresa, they can deliver the outcome the soul desires. A true awakening.

I had found my Ravenna gelateria, at last. It was *biologico*, that is, organic, so it was, you know, healthy. It was called Dolce Bio and was on busy Via Trieste, quite some distance out of the centre, so the extra cycling out there and back meant I really wasn't taking on any calories at all. They hand-made their ice cream daily, so the selection was small but the taste immense. For seating, they had planks set up running between pot plants and crates. They faced into the store, appearing like pews, with the reverential all lined up there, slurping, speechlessly giving praise to the man at the refrigerated high altar of goodness. Each time I left there I died a little, knowing it would be the last time I would have that *exact* creation. *Mamma mia.* No unnatural nothing and oodles of deliciousness. I forgave the man behind the counter his uncertain standoffishness, which wasn't his fault. He didn't get too many non-Italian-speaking, over-excited, quite possibly drooling, bike-riding Australians at his counter, of that I was sure.

My alarm went off at 6.30 a.m. so I could catch the eight o'clock train to Bologna for a day visit. That beautiful university city is a busy one, especially compared to the pace of life in the centre of Ravenna, where cars were limited, many of my days were spent lying on the beach reading, and gelato was back to being my main concern—other than Lord Byron.

I was walking down Bologna's colonnaded streets between the buzzing and grand university buildings when I realised I was done with sightseeing for now. I was a bit tired of being the unfamiliar element. I wondered about Lord Byron, who had spent his time there, and his wanderlust, his constant need for new experience, new inspiration. I did think he was running. Who knew from what? Probably not from the things everyone believed he was, least of all from the things *he* might have thought he was.

This I would soon come to know about myself.

I had a ticket to another Ravenna Festival event. I was contemplating not going. It began at 9.30 p.m. and my day in Bologna had taken it out of me. At the Bologna university's *pinacoteca* I'd seen a few great Tintoretto works and then I'd been privy to a room full of exemplary Raphaels. I'd stood as close as I could without the alarm going off, trying to see his brush strokes. I honestly couldn't. The faces, the unfiltered humanity: how did he commit to eternity like that? He made Tintoretto look like an artisan. So I'd had me some art for the day.

But my festival ticket, to the soloists of the Vienna Philharmonic, was a gift from the festival director. So not going would have been rude. I was on my way out the door for some pre-concert dinner when my phone sounded. It was a message from Paul. 'Just got back to town from the office. Are you free for a bite?'

'Dolce Bio is my place for gelato too!' said Paul as we ate a tasty dinner at one of Ravenna's crazy good *trattorie*. 'I can't believe I haven't seen you there.' If he knew the amount of time I'd been spending at the place, his incredulity would have been ten-fold. 'My friend who took me there is a Sicilian. He says it's the best he's had.'

'Outside Sicily, surely,' I chimed in.

'Well, no, he said best, full-stop.'

'Wow. Do I know gelato, or what?' I was very impressed with myself.

Paul laughed.

We talked more of the places we'd both been, the experiences we'd had there, two lives lived on the move. But mostly we talked about Italy. When you share a common love of *bella Italia*, conversation is endless, like her charms.

'Gosh, look at the time. I have to go to the theatre,' I said.

'I must say I'm jealous of you going to a concert,' he replied. 'Do you think they'll have any tickets left?'

We walked up to Ravenna's ornate Teatro Alighieri where the box office did indeed still have some tickets. Paul bought one and then we went to the concert, sat together and enjoyed it, but enjoyed more our riffing at interval on the theme of what would make a young man pick up the harp and become so brilliant at it as the fellow from the Vienna Phil who was the star of the show. 'I mean,' I said, 'I could be brilliant at the harp but I've never encountered one. How on earth does one get interested in the harp?'

'I know. Football or the harp. Exactly when does a young man make that choice? Guitar or football, I understand. Both have a certain swagger to them and you have to choose one or the other to be any good, I suppose. Guitar or the harp I understand, if you happen to be anywhere there's a harp. Though it's not an altogether manly instrument. Maybe he began at school playing the guitar and progressed to that big thing with lots of strings in the corner of the music room. Maybe it's a progressive process to get to the harp.'

'Like all things in life, really. I wasn't born liking black coffee. It evolved through choices and exposure,' I said. 'I guess like being single at our age. Did either of us choose it? Nope, right?'

Paul was silent.

'We evolved into that,' I continued.

'Hey, would you like a prosecco?' he offered.

'No thanks, just a water,' I said. 'But I'll happily watch you drink one.'

After the concert we strolled to nearby Piazza del Popolo, Ravenna's main town square, which has been called one of the finest in Italy, a much-loved space with layers of the city's history in its exquisite architecture, and where late into the evening, especially if it's warm, the Ravennese love to congregate, stroll, cycle, talk, sit. We walked to a place there where they served gelato out of a hole in the wall. It was no Dolce Bio, but it was convenient. And still good. Hey, it was Italian ice cream in Italy.

And then, with a kiss on the cheek for me from him,

we parted, him going in one direction, me the other. He was lovely, I thought as I walked home. Did I have expectations? I told myself no. It was all so easy and comfortable. It was, I thought, a result of the way I was now presenting to the world—a sign that I'd shifted.

The next afternoon, Luciana came to the table outside my apartment with things for tea. No language, she said, so let's have tea. We managed some good conversation though. Charades, my disjointed Italian and Luciana's determination to tell me her stories were a potent mix. She made this crazy concoction in her cup of massive chunks of lemon and weak tea and dissolved biscuits. '*Zuppa di te*,' she said, and we both cracked up. Tea soup. She told me she was off to a wedding in Tuscany on the weekend. That the little shih tzu was not eating, which was news to me because he may have been a bit blind but he had the olfactory abilities of a bloodhound and every night I cooked chicken, steak or lamb, he was sharing half my dinner. Perhaps this was why he was not eating the dry food Luciana fed him. And she told me that since I'd been in Ravenna, compared to how I had looked when I arrived, I was looking healthier and happier. She told me in Italian and I understood.

Later that night I went to see *Matthew Bourne's Dorian Gray*, which was in town as part of the festival. It was a powerful take on hedonism, a reminder of how you could be enjoying yourself but if you were only into the beauty of your own existence with no eye on the bigger picture, it could easily slip into dark chaos. Intending to keep God close was no insurance policy because you could kid yourself you were doing that. Honest self-examination was the only failsafe, I thought.

After the show I went back to the hole-in-the-wall gelato place, put my two euro in the tray and ordered from the same woman who had served Paul and me.

'Where your husband?' the lady said as she scooped. I laughed. 'You his wife from England? He say his wife no come. And here you are.'

I found the strength to nod and laugh again. And then I sat down on one of the benches in Piazza del Popolo to eat my gelato. But for the first time ever, I had no appetite for it.

Deep down somewhere I had known this. Though I could have misunderstood the woman, and though Paul wore no ring and only spoke in singular terms of his experiences, which family people tended not to do, instead using the more inclusive 'we', his decision to live in a serviced apartment in Ravenna and his wistfulness at all the things I had done in the city had made me fleetingly suspect he might have flown home on weekends. 'It's so sad. I go to work, come home and don't really get to experience all these things,' he had said. The suspicion had arisen. I'd batted it off, choosing to ignore it.

Some little boys were playing soccer in the *piazza* and I sat watching them, out late at night, running like their lives depended on it, their wayward kicks no cause for ridicule from their friends. They would improve. They all knew that. The ball would go near grown men who would kick it back to the little ones, knowing it too. A communion from man to boy.

One little guy, he wasn't allowed to play. I noticed him as he stood, in his high-hiked short pants, watching the big boys, his hands on his hips, his little bowl-cut head watching every curve of the ball. He didn't give in though. He ran with them, followed them, got a touch when he could, when someone was kicking for the imaginary goal post and it was the more the merrier along the imaginary defence line.

Then all of the older kids bar the one who owned the ball had to go home. And the little kid got to kick back and forth then with the ball's owner. A girl all dressed in pink with a ruffled skirt and cardigan, and only very recently walking so she still needed to hold her father's hands to do so, wanted a kick. The boys let her. She squealed every time she laid her foot on the ball. She kicked better than she walked. It was sweet watching the little boy with the high pants and the bowl cut. He wanted to keep playing with the bigger boy. He included the little girl but he was itching to keep kicking as big as he could go. You could see how torn he was. His heart was on his sleeve.

And then the kid who owned the ball left the square and went home. And the little bowl-cut boy put his hands in his pockets and wandered off, despondent.

That little boy, he was trying and trying and trying. Trying to be what he wanted to be in this world, wanting desperately to be part of life and have his turn. His little lost face on the sidelines and his eagerness when he was included, when he was thrown a bone, that's what it was about him that ultimately made me see the truth about myself.

I had been watching that kid for an hour. Now he was gone, the square still full of Saturday night people coming and going from restaurants and bars, strolling with ice cream, standing smoking cigarettes and talking, seemed so empty.

I sat undistracted. I didn't move, didn't try to get the attention of passing dogs or children like I usually did. Didn't pull out the notebook. I just sat. And then I saw me, trying, trying, trying, and there, in the square, finally done trying.

I saw me and I didn't flinch. I didn't look away. I sat and looked at me. I was me, only me. The sound and activity dissipated. I stopped being anything but me.

And I found my grief.

It wasn't grief for Paul being married. My grief was for the wife and mother I would never be. I'd spent twenty years pretending I didn't care about that, that I was fine. There was this rule, I thought, among single women of a certain age, a rule dictated to us—by whom? Me, really—that it wasn't okay to lament missing out on those things. That as a career woman with freedom and a mind and independent means, I was some kind of traitor if I looked back and said, well sure, but I might have liked …

I tried to turn my thoughts of this into thoughts of regret, but they were not that. I tried to use them to invalidate the way my life was now, but they would not let me do that either. There was no using them for anything other than the purity of what they were, an acceptance of the finality of my situation in relation to marriage and motherhood and of the factors that brought me to it. My dad, my mum, my choices.

I grieved for everything that I had to give that I hadn't been able to. I had an ocean of love to give. And I grieved for the end of the struggle. The busyness, the effort, the chirpiness, the lipstick, the making myself ready for him, and then, the ever increasing panic that this was all passing me by, and then the alcohol, more busyness, effort, chirpiness, lipstick, and ever more alcohol to try harder, and harder still, and then more busyness, effort, chirpiness, lipstick, alcohol …

I really wanted this thing, this marriage and motherhood thing. And it was not okay that it didn't happen. It was not okay in the way it was not okay to have my mum die when I was relatively young. It was as final as death. This denial of being that young mum and wife I always assumed I would be and always thought I would be so good at; it could not be reversed. No amount of beseeching God could change it. It was gone. It was the death of a huge part of me. I saw that now.

I didn't before this night.

Of course I could still get married. But that wasn't all of it. There it was too, the bigger pain of not having what others had. And of thinking myself substandard because I had not been picked.

And now I knew why I did what I did, why I drank the way I did.

I stopped pretending to myself, right there, right then. I stopped running. Completely.

Three days later, the following Monday, my last full day in Ravenna, I rode my bike past Palazzo Guiccioli, waved at Lord Byron and then took my trusty steed back to Signor Luciano Sambi. I cried when I had to leave it. It had become such a part of me. The *signori* in the workshop, Sambi included, got a laugh out of the parting scene.

Around 3 p.m. I checked my phone. There was a message from Paul. It had lobbed four hours earlier. He asked if I was still in Ravenna and did I want to have dinner. Of course I was there. He knew that. I kind of knew I would hear from him on my last day in town. Nice and safe. Married, for sure. But I said yes out of curiosity.

We arranged to meet in Piazza del Popolo at 8 p.m. When I saw him from a distance, there was a hunched defeat to him that I hadn't noticed before. We decided to dine at Cappello, a busy wine bar and bistro around the corner from my place, right across the street from the market. We sat outdoors and the conversation burbled along, but I could see his pain. He had the discomfort of duplicity, no question. We basically talked again about everything I had done in Ravenna in contrast to everything he hadn't due to work. I kept it bright. Didn't let on.

Halfway through dinner he got a text message and the mood at the table changed. He began sweating, looked ill, commented on the heat of the evening. It was actually balmy.

And then he said by way of explaining the message, 'I'm always managing crises at work. It never stops.'

I knew there was a crisis but it had nothing to do with work.

And then he mentioned that he had flown back to the UK on the weekend just passed. Yep, married. I felt sorry for him then, which was a patronising emotion that I tried not to indulge in. But I couldn't help it. I saw that I was, to him, an exotic, interesting bird that had flown out of nowhere onto his windowsill. He didn't want to let it inside, but he did want to look at it awhile. In the end, he hadn't done anything that wrong, other than play with my heart. And in doing so, he'd revealed to me the core of the story of why I had drunk the way I did.

I was thankful.

After a post-prandial *passegiata*, he suggested another drink. The old nightcap; I used to be a great champion of it. I enjoyed the wine at dinner, I genuinely did. But I had a lemon squash for that nightcap. It was nearing midnight and I had an early train to catch the next morning.

I left him in Piazza del Popolo and to his life. I didn't think he wanted to complicate his existence and neither did I.

I walked out of that square for the final time, down the little side street that led to mine, Via Paolo Costa. Music emanated from the top floor of one of the fifteenth-century *palazzi*. It was a tenor and a soprano singing transcendently to exquisitely played piano. It took me a minute because my mind went to Elvis and 'It's Now or Never'—but they were singing 'O Sole Mio'.

I laughed. I leaned against a wall, listening, gazing up to the windows of the top floor of that *palazzo*, thrown open on that perfect summer evening, with lights blazing down into the otherwise quiet, dark street. Yes, I was still 'solo', as I used to think that lyric said. But now I knew it was really about the sun and I was seeing the light now. When the singers finished, the gathering they sang to erupted into bravos.

'*Bravissimo!*' I called out, though they wouldn't have heard. And anyway, I was saying it to me.

17

Pisa

I have looked out
In the vast desolate night in search of him;
I watched for what I thought was him coming; for
With fear rose longing in my heart to know
What 'twas which shook us all—but nothing came!

Cain

Transplanting to Pisa, where Percy and Mary Shelley were now living, Lord Byron also had the company of Teresa's family, exiled from Ravenna, as well as a band of Englishmen for whom literary aspirations and a liking for how they saw themselves in Byron's reflected glory were motivation enough to be in the city. Lord Byron now led a life free of the social whirl in which he'd indulged. His daily pursuits—an expat salon of poetry readings and planning for a new magazine, picking oranges from his garden, his sporting activities of riding, shooting and billiards, and gossiping about fellow countrymen and country with those who knew both intimately—were, for a while, halcyon. After some friction over Allegra's wellbeing and the general attraction-repulsion effect of two brilliant spirits enmeshed, Shelley and Byron reconnected on a simple level of friendship, spending happy, creative times together, as they had back in Geneva.

It was not long, though, before consequence caught up with Lord Byron. If we do reap as we sow, then Lord Byron's Tuscan crop had been fertilised with the sense of destiny that had followed him since boyhood. His attraction to Greece, from his classical studies at Harrow and Cambridge, had already been realised as an essential part of his being when he spent idyllic days in Athens on his first lot of travels. 'Greece has ever been for me, as it must be for all men of any feeling or education, the promised land of valour, of the arts, and of liberty throughout the ages,' he wrote. Now, only a couple of years more than a decade but lifetimes of experience later, Lord Byron was longing for his own spiritual promised land, his inner place where valour, art and liberty, the things that mattered to him, remained pure and unadulterated; where they were all that was, and the opinions and expectations of others fell away. A series of events would spur him to actively seek that inner realm. And given his stated feelings about Greece, it would be the obvious place to which he would turn, the country's war the obvious theatre in which to carry out his last quest.

But he would stay awhile in Pisa before that final chapter. Even then, when Lord Byron was there in the early 1820s, Pisa was a strange little city, almost directly across the top of Italy's boot from Ravenna and, like Ravenna, almost at the seaside but not quite. It was unbelievably humid in summer, cold and damp in winter and, at the time, sparsely populated between its unusual monuments and curious tower. Lord Byron turned to writing more and more in his large *palazzo* on the River Arno. There was a sense of urgency to it, all-night sessions fuelled by alcohol. What caused that urgency he never stated. Perhaps it was premonition.

With the publication of a new work, *Cain*, he caused more outrage among England's pious, who now accused him of being an evil and cold-blooded atheist. In many respects, it was the final nail in the coffin of his reputation. He had weathered all manner of accusations, but questioning the existence of God was going too far.

The Tuscan authorities, meanwhile, wanted him and his adopted family, the trouble-making Gambas, out of their province. There were run-ins with police, detainment of members of their staff and altercations in the street.

Then a terrible succession of events began.

Back in England, Byron's mother-in-law died. The date: 28 January 1822. Though he hated the woman, and her death meant more income for him, he suffered nevertheless. In her will she had stipulated that a portrait of her son-in-law be kept away from her grandchild, Ada, till she was twenty-one. The symbolic arrow hit its target, Lord Byron's heart, squarely.

He was as good as dead to one daughter. It was only three months later that the other, Allegra, succumbed to fever on 20 April 1822. The depression he was already feeling over Ada made his despair at the death of Allegra exponentially deeper.

Less than three months later, on 8 July, Percy Shelley was out on the boat known as the *Don Juan* off the coast near Viareggio when something catastrophic occurred. The boat went missing. A week on, Shelley's decomposed body washed ashore and was buried in the sand by authorities.

A month later, Byron and a small group of his expat cronies dug Shelley's corpse out of the sand and cremated him on the shore. It remains one of the seminal moments in Romantic imagery. But for Byron, living it, the pain was real. This was not, for him, a grand gesture of genre. It was a horrible end to a connection between two soul mates. It's said that, rather than stand by the funeral pyre with his cloak billowing in the coastal wind, as was portrayed in a famous painting of the scene, Lord Byron didn't stick around. He swam vigorously out into the deep ocean as the fire blazed and returned when it had died down.

Within a couple of months of that, Byron would pack for Genoa, from where he would leave Italy for the final time.

My reading of the spiritual dilemma facing the central character in Lord Byron's *Cain* is quite opposite to that of those who pilloried him. One of the things I truly knew in my search for God was that when I was fearfully longing for God's help I was as far away from knowing him as I could possibly be. When I was feeling desolate it was a sure sign that I had abandoned myself. Nothing ever came in that state.

I thought Byron's lines were implicitly pregnant with the knowledge that when one was *not* seeking and longing fearfully, when we were moving through our dark night in submission, that was when we truly knew God.

Unquestioning faith might have been religion's ideal. But it was Christianity's own Saint John of the Cross who first coined the term 'the dark night' to describe the period in which the soul travelled painfully questioning. He did so in the sixteenth century, well before Byron referenced 'the vast desolate night'. Eighteen hundred years before Byron, Jesus asked why his God had forsaken him.

I thought Lord Byron showed true spirituality: a preparedness to examine and experience God, in both the negative and the positive, the presence and the absence, and the presence *in* the absence. And I thought he showed a faith, nothing blind about it, in the notion that in the end, life—and death—had to have meaning.

It made me sad that he was so vilified, so misunderstood.

*

The day before I was to travel on the Florence–Livorno line there had been a terrible train crash. People died. I had taken a train from Ravenna to Bologna, and changed for Florence, from where I was to set out for Pisa. When I got to that bustling, nerve-wracking, grand station, Firenze Santa Maria Novella, all the trains on the Livorno line were cancelled due to a sudden strike over safety issues. Hanging onto my bags for dear life, sweating in the way only thwarted plans can cause, and trying to keep an eye out for thieving gypsies, I studied the board clacking over with departures and arrivals. Seeing there was a train leaving for Lucca any minute, I jumped on it. It was a risk. I didn't know if a train ran between Lucca and Pisa, but I figured it was worth getting closer—Lucca and Pisa are about thirty kilometres apart. I could be hanging around in Florence for who knew how long. Well, I lumbered onto that train, rather than jumped. My bags and me: the never-ending story.

The Lucca line had its own set of issues. My train stopped halfway between Florence and its final stop, Viarregio, as there were some safety concerns with a train coming the other way. We saw it eventually, surrounded by firemen having a good look at it. Better safe than sorry, given the terrible event of the day before.

While Italy could be profoundly inefficient in some aspects, the country's trains were fabulous, save the occasional strike. But the roll through the Tuscan countryside on this day after disaster was snail pace. Dazzling though, especially after the flat unchanging landscapes I'd been used to for the couple of months prior. All those hills and castles and mountain hamlets, Tuscany sure was blessed in the looks department. I had grown to love that sprawling countryside of the Veneto and Emilia Romagna coast, but my eyes were like saucers trying to take in Tuscany. I'd seen it before but driven it alone, spending most of my time looking at the blacktop on the *autostrada*. The train, especially a slow-moving one, offered a cinemascope movie view of it.

Pisa was hot when I arrived mid-afternoon. Well, it was July in northern Italy. I hauled my bags down Corso Italia, the city's main shopping strip, and arrived at the River Arno that divides Pisa in two. It was essentially not much different along there now to Byron's time: those squat, colourful buildings, with their uniformly green shutters, unbroken lines of them lining the river's wide seeming stagnancy, almost perfectly reflected in that stillness. There is a strangeness to the way the Arno looks in Pisa, and it is because of the lack of greenery. Though the Tuscan hills are in the background in some spots, in the centre of Pisa, the riverbank has been built out completely, not a tree in sight. I crossed it at busy Ponte di Mezzo and was stunned to be met by a large statue of Garibaldi that looked for all the world like my dad. It was quite disconcerting, the tight protruding belly, the beard and moustache. There was something in the attitude of this statue—the hand on one hip that tilted out and skyward, one leg forward provocatively, the arrogance, defiance, vanity, the potency—that was pure Bryan Jameson.

My home for my stay turned out to be one of Pisa's most photographed buildings outside the Piazza dei Miracoli: the Palazzo Agostini, a fifteenth-century elaborately detailed terracotta ormnament a minute on foot down the road from Dad/Garibaldi, right on the banks of the Arno. I did not have river views. I was to the back of the building, in a spacious studio that was as high as it was square, with soaring ceilings. It had three huge shuttered windows overlooking an ancient alleyway and a building that showed the layers of renovation, from medieval to Renaissance to Byron's time. There was a pillar in the corner of my combined lounge-dining-bedroom that was the original deal, nearly 600 years old. I stood with my hand on it for I don't know how long. It hummed.

Downstairs was the Caffè dell'Ussero, a legendary hangout of intellectuals, writers, scientists and artists since the 1700s. Apparently not Lord Byron, but it was still excellent to know.

The owners had organised a bicycle for me and I jumped on to investigate town. The road along the Arno was busy with cars, buses and trucks, and the pedestrian action was thick and chaotic, quite different to the ordered mayhem of Ravenna where I did not have to mix it up with cars much at all. Frazzled, I stopped in a bar along the river. There was a hardness to Pisa that I picked up on immediately, something I had not figured on encountering at all. It was Tuscany, the dreamiest of Italian locations. But there was a sort of pugnacity to Pisa, maybe as a result of being so outshone by the likes of exquisite Florence, Lucca and San Remo. It was not an immediately endearing place.

The bar was owned by one of the most handsome men I had ever had the pleasure of conversing with. He had jet-black hair, long but not too long, Keanu Reeves kind of bone structure, a nice crinkle at the eye, a well-trimmed beard. Not a dandy, but well put together in a casual, youthful way.

'You are from Australia!' His English was better than he thought it was. I put him at thirty-five at the oldest. 'I love Australia. I must go there.'

'You should go!' I said, munching on one of the delectable sandwiches his bar served. 'Go to Sydney. All the single men are gay.' Singing from my same old songbook, still. 'You'd do great with the ladies. Assuming you're straight,' I added. But he would do pretty well with the blokes, too. He'd have a full dance card before he disembarked.

'All gay? That is a shame.'

'Not a shame, a tragedy,' I laughed.

'A tragedy, yes! My ex-girlfriend. She went to live in ... I forget where it was. I can't remember the name, but it is in America and it is the island of the gay.'

I cracked up now. 'Where is the island of the gay? I need to know!'

It turned out to be Key West. But he wasn't finding the conversation at all hilarious. Italian straight men did seem to find the whole gay male business somewhat confounding. Not in any judgmental way or with any hatred, in my experience. It was a concept these absolutely women-oriented men found impossible to get their head around.

And I know I shouldn't have laughed at anyone else's abuse of language, which I was with my amusement at the 'island of the gay' line, because I had taken to making things up. It had been so long since I heard long brackets of the sound of my own voice. So I had started to say things in a made-up Italian that I thought approximated what I wanted to say. I mean, our language was Latin based, put an 'o' on the end, a little 'issima' here and there ... I had a number I liked, it was *ventisette* (twenty-seven). I threw it into conversation just because I liked it. I eventually realised that when I said, '*Mi dispiace, no cambio*', meaning to tell people in shops and cafés that I was very sorry but I did not have any change when I handed over a fifty euro note, I was actually apologising for not changing.

I also worked out that the word Luciana kept saying to me, 'beachy', which I took as cute slang for the beach, was not what I thought. Thinking it was an English word the Italians had adopted, similar to how they had the word 'shopping' for instance, I'd started saying 'beachy' back to her and to others in Ravenna, when trying to explain where I had been for the day. 'Beachy, beachy,' I would say, when I'd been lying flat on my back on a banana lounge by the Adriatic. But Luciana was actually saying *bici*, which is Italian for bicycle. They really must have thought I was obsessed with that bike, riding it all day, '*bici, bici*', when I was actually lying on the beach.

The bar owner might not have found the conversation funny, but he found another pleasure in it. 'I like you,' he said. 'You laugh. Laugh is good. A smiling lady is a good lady. What you do here in Pisa?'

I told him.

'These dead men, they interest Italy. We learn from them. They are our fathers. You learn from this man?'

'I have learned from this man,' I said quietly.

'What have you learned? Something about Italy?'

'*Si*,' I brightened up. 'That men take many lovers in Italy.'

'*Nooooo*,' he did that long Italian negative, with a turn of the head and a hand raised dramatically. 'We find the right woman, we love her and her only. Maybe this thing you learned, about men taking many lovers, you learned about the Englishman in Italy, not about Italy. And maybe you learn from your mother and father, that this is not so desirable.'

'I did learn that from my father, but not in the way you mean,' I answered, wondering if he was in any way related to the *signora* in Padua who had also asked me about life lessons.

'Ah,' he answered. I was quite sure he didn't get what *I* meant. 'So what did you get from him, your father? Did you get this laugh?'

It was such an immense question. The laugh, I think that was from my mother. From my father: who I was? I thought then, faced with the question probably for the first time, that the answer was who I was not.

'In his lifetime, I thought I got nothing,' I said to this man. 'But in the past few years, since he died, I do believe I am seeing myself better, in contrast to him.'

It was a statement I know the Italian didn't understand. I was only now awakening to myself.

My father was dying for a long time. He would call us on the phone at Lavender Street. We, meaning Erin and I, the youngest children and at the centre of our parents' tug-o-war, would hate picking up to him. He would ask us to come and see him. I couldn't begin to think how that could happen so I wouldn't even consider it. His soft, cigarette-shredded voice would sound drunken, slurry. He'd go on. I didn't remember about what because I was a kid and there was something on the television in the other room. The phone was in the kitchen, and in those days, phones were fixed-line analogue. Erin's evil budgie, Noddy, named after the lead singer of Slade, her favourite band, was in a cage above the phone, and not only could he imitate the phone perfectly, but when you were on it he would shower you with seed.

'Come and see me,' Dad would say. Showers of seed. TV studio audience laughing in the other room. Damn, what had I missed? Our loyalty to our mother was cement. We had been let down by him so many times. His no-shows, his embarrassing, scandalous flirting with any female he wasn't related to if he did actually show and there was some kind of gathering on. It was the way he was, the person he was.

And now he needed us. But it didn't sound like he needed us. I didn't even consider that either. It sounded like another game. Phone up the girls and keep them away from the telly.

He'd want to talk to Mum too. Try and be friends. Can't we just ... The born-again Catholic wanting absolution.

I also believed he loved her. Or remained connected to

her spiritually. Six kids over twenty years. They didn't come from playing Monopoly. The complexity of human emotion; they had been kids together, bringing up kids. They knew each other from their teen years. No one had that with him except his brother Kevin and my aunty Phil, his much younger brother Bernard and Bernard's wife Elaine. It was important for me to consider this.

But she would never forgive him and neither would we. And he never really had any humility. It was a two-way street that our entire existence relied on, this tension created by our opposition to each other.

Plus, we believed him to be crying wolf. That cancer, it went on for so many years. Mum told us he was crying wolf. We believed her. And still he smoked Camel non-filter and drank a lot and took wild expeditions into the Australian outback in his orange Nissan Patrol with the bullhorns attached to the front. He didn't seem to behave like a sick man. He was going to outlive all of us with this alleged illness.

I can't recall who told us he was beyond doubt on his way out. But someone did. Vera, our sister-in-law, drove Erin and me out to Romsey, which was in the country then but is part of Melbourne suburbia now, where he'd bought a house and where he was now in a private hospital, dying. For real this time.

I remember the shiny linoleum floor and the cool, dark, country hospital hallway, the quiet. A crucifix somewhere.

And seeing him. My God, seeing him, determined to appear lucid, that gaunt, sunken, wide-eyed version of the ferociously alive man we knew. There was a packet of Camel plain and a tray of empty oyster shells on the table wheeled across him. He seemed, I don't know, annoyed? Resentful? Like our presence made it real, finally, to him. And yet it was all strangely dispassionate.

It was Good Friday.

I told him I loved him, but back then, I wouldn't have known I did. I just wanted to hear him say it back. He didn't. But he did say, in a voice that wasn't the voice I knew, 'I'm very proud of you.' I resented that. I do see now that I got more than any of my other brothers and sisters did.

He was only in his early sixties.

The night he died was Easter Sunday. Erin, Bernadette, Mum and I had that second sat down to dinner when the call came. 'Well,' we all said. And kept eating. It was some big night at the Metro, a then swish nightclub on Bourke Street in Melbourne. You should still go, of course you should, Mum told us. We went—even Bernadette, a decade older than Erin and me, who had shared adult conversations with Mum long before we had. I wonder what Mum went through alone that night.

I would do all this so differently now.

At the last minute, Mum decided to come to the funeral. My dad's second wife had asked me to tape-record the service because I was still working at ABC Radio news at the time, as was she. I had to lug this big old-time tape unit and microphone and stand with me. Someone else should have done that. That I should work at my father's funeral, now I think about it, put me outside the experience.

But we *were* outside the experience. So many of the people at that funeral figured they knew who we were in his life, and what that meant. We were his children, so they said all the sympathetic things you say to kids who have lost their beloved dad. He was our father, so they sang his praises as if we knew and loved him the way they did. It was so terrifically apparent that those people didn't know the real picture of how he had abandoned his kids and how bitter relations were and I just didn't have it in me to pop that bubble. In fact, I rather liked the play-acting, pretending I was the dutiful daughter for the day, not some semi-stranger to the deceased. But underneath it all I was desperate for acknowledgment of my pain, and feeling oh so embarrassed and very much on the outer of it all.

Mum did not go to the house for the wake but held court all afternoon at the pub across the way. The old timers who knew her, plus the boys—our brothers—and us girls, we did shifts over there with her. When it came time to leave late in the night, she and the other woman came face-to-face. It was the other woman's idea. Mum dropped to her knees and wailed like a Middle-Eastern mother who'd just lost her son to a bullet. It was awful. The boys bundled her into the car. It was never, ever mentioned again. Even in the car on the way home.

We didn't mention stuff. Like I said, I would do this differently now.

I still felt disconnected to his death. Unlike Mum's, which came like a hurricane, and still sat next to me every minute of every day like the space where a lost limb used to be, this just came and went.

As I rode back to my apartment, past Dad/Garibaldi, I wondered, twenty-two years after his death, was I following a man like Lord Byron to try to understand a man like my father? Charismatic, loved by and lover of a multitude, passionate, political, selfish, creative, courageous, a cad.

Had I not become the wife and mother I had wanted to be because of him? Or was this not his fault at all? Had I not become that wife and mother because I had not faced up to who he was and what he was? Because I had not grieved him? I didn't know him but had I craved to? Is this why men who were aspects of him kept coming into my life? The cruelty, emotional unavailability, philandering? Is this why Lord Byron was really in my life now? I couldn't deal with the nitty-gritty of my dad's life, like the other child out there somewhere. So had I chosen to examine a life encapsulating his energy and character, an arm's length handling of the material?

I heard the cosmic kerplunk. And then my soul let out a long, exhausted, relieved sigh.

18

Mario

'I have come from my rest to him I love best
That I may be happy, and he may be bless'd.
I have pass'd the guards, the gate, the wall;
Sought thee in safety through foes and all.'

The Siege of Corinth

A month after Shelley's death, Lord Byron was packing up his
Pisan *palazzo* and posse for Genoa, the Ligurian port city to the
north. He felt strongly that his time in Italy was up and that he
needed to 'leave more than a mere name; and besides that, to be
able to do good to others to a greater extent'.

Though he was still writing profusely, he met regularly
with a Greek royal, Prince Argiropoli, who was residing in Pisa
and had come to be a source of information on the Greek War of
Independence, which had been running since 1821 in an effort
to break Hellas free of Ottoman rule.

Once in Genoa, Lord Byron met with members of the
London Greek Committee, a body seeking English support for
the Greek cause. Soon after, Lord Byron was elected to the
committee. From there, his involvement steamrolled. He was
going to Greece.

What of Teresa? She was kept in the dark, until word came

that her father was allowed back to Ravenna on the proviso that Teresa accompany him. This seemed to Lord Byron like his out. And even when she was finally given the news of Lord Byron's imminent departure, it was not directly from him, but via her brother. She was, of course, inconsolable. Her choice then: whether to join a convent or live with her father.

And then he was gone.

In some ways, life seems to change on a pinhead. But it does not. Change comes like a train: distant, faint, then around the last bend and on us. Why was it necessary for him to have more to his life than poetry? Did Lord Byron look back at his years of excess in Italy and feel the need for penance? It might have been a creeping disquiet. The kind that, one day, has you wake up sick of your partner, your job and your circumstances, sick of yourself. As much as those moments look like they come out of nowhere, they do not.

Or perhaps it was a submission to destiny. A letting go. That sense that holding on to your stuff, the things by which you have defined yourself up to now, is far more dangerous than allowing yourself to free-fall.

It takes courage to let go like that. It can look selfish to those invested in us remaining as we were. It can cause them, and us, pain. And it can look sudden. But it is not. It's always a gradual release. We begin it the moment we call out in our dark night. Someone is listening. And their answer, when the prayer is sincere, is the beginning.

I was having a hard time getting Pisa. It was puzzling. It was so very hot and humid. At 3 a.m. on my first night trying to sleep there, I had discovered there were four enormous communal garbage bins right outside my windows. Pisans apparently like to recycle and they like to do it at all hours of the night. The regular crashing of bottles into the glass bin echoing up the tiny laneway was horrific. But also comical. Who puts out their recycling at 3 a.m.?

There was light shining in all night from the student digs across the laneway. Two out of the three enormous sets of windows in my apartment had shutters. The one missing them was the one next to the bed. Of course.

Riding a bike in Pisa was frightening, though I insisted on doing it. The heat was extraordinary, the mosquitoes could fight a matador and did I mention those bloody bins stank? The garbos came several times a day and they dragged those stinking bins down that ragged, uneven bluestone lane right below my window and had loud arguments with each other while they were doing it. The sun was so bright. There was little green in the streets of downtown Pisa. It was as if the city had somehow given up on itself too, it was so unkempt. Students had taken over *piazze* and turned them into open-air beer halls. There were puddles of puke in the morning.

And yet, I was more content than I had ever been. My building backed onto a zig-zag melding of small squares that was Pisa's open-air food market and something of a restaurant quarter (perhaps explaining the extraordinary stink of the bins and the late-night depositing of bottles in them). It was lively and picturesque out there, with the providores selling brightly coloured fruits and vegetables, breads, charcuterie and cheeses from under awnings. The squares were lined with butcher shops and delis, cafés and bars in buildings that showed the layers of centuries upon centuries of history in their higgledy-piggledy brickwork. The café that I liked, Bar Lo Stuzzichiere, was in the middle of it all and had a big awning the size of a double garage out front with tables and chairs under it. I could sit there for hours and watch an endless parade of entertaining characters. It was fantastic.

One of the great things about Italy is that you can stare. It is totally fine. It's a national pastime. Whether you are a starer or staree, it is completely acceptable. Expected, even. I'd reacted badly in the past to being the staree. Now I declared myself open for staring season. There was a dear old couple who came to Lo Stuzzichiere every night and ordered a half-litre bottle of water between them, then partook generously of the *apertivo*-hour bar snacks. And then they stared, like they were watching telly. I was their prime viewing some nights, and when I was, I felt honoured.

I had become papier-mâché after a number of years on this earth, bits of newsprint and coloured paper clogged together over my originality. Each time the world told me my true self was in some aspect defective I stuck new bits on to mask myself. And then I was so patched up I bore no resemblance to the real thing. The second I made a decision to stop drinking like I was, the process began to reverse. At the risk of working a metaphor too hard, drinking, smoking and drugs, but drinking in particular, had been the hard lacquer setting all that paper into place, a thick impermeable glaze that ensured no more hurt could be added, but none could fall off either.

In Pisa, I sensed I'd got rid of all that. I felt more authentic than I ever had. I was sitting outside little Bar Lo Stuzzichiere when I became aware of what I *wasn't* feeling, and hadn't for a while. That searching for him, I was no longer doing that. And that discomfort, that mistrust of myself, it was gone too. I'd dropped that stuff somewhere along the way. Well, when I thought about it, I knew where it had fallen away. It had peeled off in Ravenna, in Piazza del Popolo, where I'd found that from which I'd been running. I looked back and saw the immense battle I'd fought. And yet the victory had been so simple, so small. But like a tiny little well-aimed pebble thrown with velocity, it had shattered my prism, decimating the distortion of self-deception. I'd been able to drink some wine with dinner in Pisa and delight in it for its own sake. No compulsion, no need, no craving: just simple enjoyment of one of life's pleasures. And yes, I had stopped sizing up every male in the vicinity for suitability. I had found my clarity.

Pisa is awash with awesome *trattorie*, little neighbourhood joints that with loving care honour Tuscany's delicious bounty. Da Cucciola, over on the other side of the Arno from where I was staying, was owned by Graziella, who decided to sit with me and get her waitress to be the interpreter in our conversation. She was a spritely seventy-year-old who loved *la musica*, loud, preferably salsa, by the sounds from the kitchen. And beer. She loved beer. When the restaurant was quiet and she was not cooking, nor sitting with me, she came and leaned on the bar with a tankard of the stuff, the vessel almost bigger than her tiny self.

She'd cooked in that restaurant for forty years. '*Bella* Julietta,' she said to me over and over. She was dismayed—she told me through the waitress—that Pisa's once-noble squares had been trashed by the students. But she was delighted when I told her, again through the waitress, that though, yes, many of Pisa's charms were faded, I'd had perhaps the best food ever in that city. And that her *coniglio alla Cacciatora*, a rabbit stew with sweet small olives and a tangy *pomodoro* sauce, was the best meal of the lot.

I was back at the Keanu lookalike's bar. 'The light is very intense in Pisa. Very different to the other side of the country,' I told him. 'I was in Ravenna before here. The light is definitely softer over the other side.'

'Which is more beautiful, Ravenna or Pisa?'

I told him Pisa, but I lied.

'Florence? Do you like?'

'Not really.'

He looked troubled.

'Too many foreigners. When I'm in Italy, I want it to sound like Italy. Florence sounds like America, so many Americans! I know that my not speaking Italian is contributing to that whole not sounding Italian thing. I get that it is hypocritical. But this is why I don't like Florence. It's *Rinascimento* Disneyland.'

He laughed heartily at this.

'But perhaps I should give Florence another chance. My head was in a bad place when I went there.' It was true. One of the reasons I was not fond of Florence was one woman's refusal to give me any table, let alone an outside one, at lunchtime because I was on my own. But it was my mum's birthday, the day I missed her most, and only a couple of months after the magazine debacle. I was in an awful headspace. Sometimes our impression of a place can be greatly coloured by what is going on inside our noggins.

'You must. Perhaps we can go there together. I will show you the lovely there.'

'Well, I would love you to show me the lovely.' I was beginning to have a silly little crush on Keanu. Not that I was looking. He just made me go a bit girly.

I hadn't found my Pisan gelato shop, but my, there was some good eating there. In one day but over several visits to Salza dal 1898, one of the oldest bars in Pisa, I had enjoyed a really very okay gelato and also a *schecherato*, a black coffee shaken deliciously with ice and sugar and poured frothy into a cocktail glass. I had an excellent *occhi di bue* cookie with the *schecherato* also. And in the evening a glass of prosecco, accompanied by potato crisps, olives and little sandwiches, all of which came for the price of the drink. How was I not the size of a house?

I went for a ride around Pisa, admiring squares and churches. It actually did have some loveliness, here and there, and green too. The big green of course, was the Campo dei Miracoli, where perfectly kept grass tied the leaning tower, baptistery and cathedral together. That cathedral, *mamma mia*, it is an extraordinary space. I was far more impressed with it than that tower. But hardly any of the Pisan churches were open to the public, which didn't help the city's image at all. I did find some enchanting corners of this secretive little city. But it hid its gems, curling around them protectively for the most part, keeping them for locals. Lovely. Confounding though. It was as if it was saying, here you go: here is our Duomo and our leaning tower. The rest, this is only for us.

Some places, it is easy to find their centre. In Venice: San Marco. In Ravenna: Piazza del Popolo. In *Roma*, well, for my money it's Piazza Navona. In Padua: Prati. In Verona: Piazza delle Erbe. I was curious to know what it was in Pisa. It was not the Piazza dei Miracoli. That was too, too touristy. I had yet to get a sense of locals there at all. There was a wonderful space, Piazza Cavalieri, flanked by Medici-era buildings but it was a thoroughfare, a crossroad for seven roads without even a roundabout. Quiet roads, fortunately. But if they put a big grassy island in the middle for people to congregate and let the traffic flow around, it would be brilliant.

Really quite confounding was Pisa.

*

Keanu was one of the sweetest handsome guys I had ever met.

I asked him about gelato. He recommended a shop called Coppelia on Piazza Cairoli where there is a statue by Leonardo da Vinci's son, Pietro. 'Very good gelato. *Artigianale*. Some gelato good but no good for you. This is natural. Good for you.'

Well then, it would be rude not to.

'My favourite is *pignolo*.'

'What is that, pine nut?'

'No, nut is *nocciolo*,' he said firmly. 'Do you like fruit or cream?'

'What's with the hard questions? I like both.'

This perplexed him, as much as the idea of the island of the gay. You were one thing or another apparently, fruit or cream. 'You go try *pignolo*.' He motioned in the direction of the gelateria, which was not far away.

I discovered there that *pignolo* was indeed pine nut. It didn't appeal. I ordered *limone* and *fragola*, my classics. I came back towards my bike, which was near the Keanu bar and saw that Keanu had sat himself down at the table I'd vacated. With a flourish, he motioned me over to sit down again.

'This is not *pignolo*.' He motioned at my ice cream. '*Allora*.' He was very disappointed.

'Excellent though,' I said through a decidedly unladylike slurp of the *artigianale* goodness.

'My name is Mario.' He said it like he was singing opera.

I introduced myself. It was about time. We'd been talking every day for quite some time now.

'Where is Romeo?'

Had I been cursed with this bloody name? I was beginning to wonder. 'It's another very good question, Mario. *Dov'è* indeed.'

'Romeo is in Australia?'

'I don't know.'

'Have you met Romeo in Italy?'

'No,' I said. 'Well, I could have.' It was true. I could have had any number of romantic assignations if I'd followed through on looks or heckles. Or perhaps, dinners. But that was not what I was looking for. And I wasn't looking any more anyway. But if I was, I'd be looking for special.

'In Australia ...' he began, and then he gave me the third degree about living there.

The next day I bought a book written by a Pisan local that contained cycling tour itineraries. Perfect. I got on my bike and followed one that appealed and in the process found an incredible church, San Francesco, and it was actually open. It is one of the most remarkable spaces I have ever seen, a fat rectangular T-bar cavern topped with six chapels and with the choir as the cross bar. It is dark and stripped back, yet rich in features such as a long walkway of tombstones, the remains of a mural by Giotto and vividly-coloured stained glass and bricks that resonate with centuries of worship. Outside there is a walled garden. It has grey gums in it. There was the strong smell of eucalyptus and crickets chirped in the heat.

Home.

I could hear traffic in there yet it was so peaceful, a very meditative place. I cried in there, purely because I was moved by that kind of beauty. But I was also asking God to help me trust in my newfound clarity. I knew, however, that the ultimate demonstration was not asking that. Trust was giving thanks, and believing in those thanks, that what you sought already was.

I did say a prayer again, for the partner that I would have one day. I knew I would find romantic love again. He could be someone like Mario, young, handsome and Italian. Someone that stunning was possible for me. This crush thing, I liked that; it meant I was willing again to be open to possibility. It had been nearly four years since I had felt anything for a man, now I was letting my head run with this Mario business. I was enjoying it. I hadn't had a pointless crush for ages. I hadn't allowed myself to. I was heartened by it for a number of reasons. I completely knew this was not reality. It was pure play. Usually, by now, at even the slightest twinge of crush, my head would have had us married and divorced and the whole box of complications to go with that, thus defeating the purpose of a crush. This could actually have been the first pure crush I had ever had.

It gladdened me on another front. I was basking in Mario's beauty rather than judging myself badly against it. I loved that there was something about him that I found a reflection of myself. And I loved that I was allowing my sense of romance even a touch out to play. It felt safe. Silly, but not ridiculous. Unlikely, but not impossible.

I was no longer threatened by my own emotions. I trusted myself to let them out for a spot of fun. And let's be honest here: after a few years without a boyfriend, it was high time I got my flirt on again.

It was, that day, also my dad's birthday. I chose to remember something nice about him, his goodnight cuddles, a hilarious, warm, spicy-smelling mix of affection and tickling. That beard was a riot. Him trying—I was also choosing to remember that. He took Erin and me to the Royal Melbourne Show every year for a number of years after my parents divorced. On one of those outings, we deliberately wandered away from him then followed him around while he looked for us. What strange children. And he took great care with Christmas presents. We were odd, wilful little girls and I think he liked our company because we were. God, he would be ninety or something now.

I still thought of him in the 1970s with all his crazy grooviness and rugged he-manliness.

He'd like to be remembered like that.

Later on his birthday, sitting in the Pisa botanic garden I thought I saw a white dove. It flew into the sun and landed on the roof of a nearby mandarin-coloured mansion. I was on a garden bench in a revelry of grief. Grief for him. I cried deep, hot, sad tears, and I felt like I was shifting some eternal sadness, a sadness of lifetimes, as if I was strong enough now for it to pass through.

I heard a voice say, '*It's time. The sadness that has been holding you back, it's time for it to pass.*'

I watched the rooftop that dove flew onto, hoping to see it again, but all that came off there were brown and grey pigeons. And I thought: a pigeon is a white dove, only with different pigment. That white dove, it was everywhere, a layer of ordinariness away from its true nature of magnificence.

I recognised that in me. I was taking my layers off to reveal my magnificence. Yes, time to let this pass.

In the evening, I rode down the north side of the River Arno heading west. There is a street called Viale delle Piagge that runs along the Arno and a strip of park, with the trees and reeds that naturally would have run all the way along once upon a time. In places, when you look across the river through the wild trees and grasses towards ancient rows of houses, you could be in another century, save for the TV antennas.

It offered a new perspective on Pisa. Air, space and green. Air and space. At last.

19

Leaving Italy

'Tis to create, and in creating live
A being more intense, that we endow
With form our fancy, gaining as we give
The life we imagine, even as I do now.

Childe Harold's Pilgrimage, Canto III

Lord Byron sold off his possessions and chartered a boat, upon which he would take medical supplies, ammunition, horses and a few good men to Greece. He had fancy uniforms made and took meetings on the terrace of his ocean-view villa, studying maps and reports from Greece. There was of course, that classic Byronic vanity to it.

Relations between Mary Shelley and Lord Byron had been terrible since the deaths of Allegra and Percy Shelley. But Mary put that behind her when the time came to farewell Byron. On 13 July 1823, she stood with Teresa as she watched a tender take the poet, Teresa's brother and six others out to the *Hercules*, the vessel that would transport them to the Ionian Islands.

But he was already gone, from Teresa and from Italy. His mind and soul had been turned towards the east for months. And though Italy would always be intrinsic to his legend, and he intrinsic to its Romantic history, Lord Byron, the poet and

Continental lover, had chosen a new life, albeit, and unbeknown to him, a brief one.

Did Lord Byron choose well in going to Greece? For the Greeks, yes. And so for the part of him, the man who 'hath no freedom to fight for at home', the answer was yes, too. For those who loved him, the answer was ambiguous. The heart breaks at loss. But true love allows the object of its devotion to do what it must do.

Goodbye is never easy, though, especially for true love.

Have I mentioned how good the food is in Pisa? I seriously had some of the best food of my life there. Seriously. The cooking was earthy and fresh and alive. It felt good for you. I thought that maybe one day, I would take a villa in the countryside not far from Pisa and come into town only to eat. But I would probably come every evening. At a garden trattoria called Al Signor Mimmo, out the back of my *palazzo*, I had a Livornese fish soup. It was strange soup (though not as strange as Luciana's *zuppa di te*) because it was almost solid. It was beyond chunky with bread and massive bits of fish, whole squids and things. There was an Irish couple at a table next to mine who ordered it and split it and the woman went all po-faced and miserable before refusing to eat it and turning away like a three-year-old. That soup was blood-rich with tomato and the seafood was one second away from still being alive. I thought it was delicious. 'It was too strong for us, we're not used to it,' her husband said apologetically to the waitress as she took it away. This is why you get bland food at tourist places.

I went to Lo Stuzzichiere to write for a while and drink coffee, went for a swim at the indoor pool—where I had to compete with about a million virile young Italian men who fancied themselves champions. I ate lunch, and felt the need for a nap. Then I got woken up by the garbos. So I yelled out the window at them—which was fine because they had no idea I was yelling at them, nor what I was saying.

Pisa might have been rough, but the Pisans were generally fantastic. There was a brilliant cast of regulars at Lo Stuzzichiere, which, by the way, meant The Teaser. There was a petite *signorina* who was a dead ringer for Pat Benatar and she was definitely *la stuzzichiere* herself. There was a loud-talking crazy guy who without hesitation marched up to people and bellowed at them merrily. Everyone brushed it off; it was so everyday for them. There was a pair of broody, black-wearing, very Hollywood indie-beauty lesbian students, with pale skin, jutting cheek bones and messy hair. Their relationship was played out for the rest of us to watch. They smoked and sulked, smouldered and smooched. A young, teetering-heeled tart with a heart was very taken with a boy living in the apartments above the café. Every morning she came and buzzed his door. Every day he ignored it. So every day she stood there, yelling his name for five minutes or so, before settling onto the stoop to wait it out. And every day, he eventually came down and let her in. There was a pair of brothers, one of whom was blind and mentally impaired, the other his devoted carer. The sightless boy would feel his pastry and cappuccino to negotiate it to his mouth and break into spontaneous giggles before yelling, '*Ciao, buongiorno!*' to anyone who approached and sometimes just to the world in general. Such inspiring joy he had.

There were market stalls down the main drag on the north side of the river most days. One of them sold Sicilian *dolce*, but also these great rice balls filled with a rich tomato, meat and pea sauce. They were crumbed and fried. They called them *arancini,* a name derived from the Italian word for orange because of their resemblance to the fruit. But they were more delicious than any orange I'd ever met. The young man who sold them to me began with the *'bella donna'* before asking me where I was from. The Australia answer was met with raptures of approval. The answer of 'single' to the question of 'are you married' was met with the jubilant suggestion that the two of us should get hitched and settle in Australia. *'Si,'* I said, *'Giovedi, te e me, chiesa di San Francesco, pomeriggio.'* Thursday, you and me, the church of Saint Francis, in the afternoon.

His mate behind the counter laughed along.

'Cambio, per favore,' I said, laughing myself. My change, please.

'One kiss! Only one kiss!'

'Cambio, you crazy Italian!'

Everyone was laughing now.

Next door to Lo Stuzzichiere was a Halal butcher. He sliced chicken breasts for me on the spot and carved off nice steaks from an eye fillet. Well, I say on the spot. Because Italian butchers do things on demand, you can wait for half an hour to be served as they lovingly prepare cuts for the people in front of you and carry out their duty of exchanging gossip and asking how everyone is. For those of us brought up in the supermarket culture, it can be excruciating. But there's no point carrying on about it. I stood patiently for twenty minutes with only one customer in front of me, which gave me time to look at what was in his refrigerated counter and join in some of the chit chat. 'What are those round things?' I asked, pointing to some plump, veiny dumplings of flesh.

'Guess what they are.' The butcher was highly amused.

'Oh my God, they are, aren't they?'

'What do you think they are?'

My face screwed up involuntarily, like the Irish lady's at the restaurant. 'What is the Italian for bull's testicles?' *Testicoli di toro*, for the record.

'You like to try?'

'Are you out of your mind?'

The butcher was delighted. 'They are *delizioso*! You come to my house, my wife cook them for you. She cooks them with breadcrumbs.'

'Though everything tastes better with breadcrumbs, and though I would love to come to your house, if you serve me bull's testicles, I will have to kill you.'

Enormous amusement I caused in the butcher shop.

On my last Sunday morning in Pisa I went to Salzi café for my coffee, and possibly the finest *cornetto crema* in Italy. I got custard over one side of my face when I bit into it. That's the result you want when you bite into a *crema*.

Sunday morning in Pisa is extra low-key because the students are all sleeping it off. I had a lane to myself at the swimming pool. As I cycled from the pool to my apartment I felt again that unfamiliar, yet completely comfortable peace which had descended on me. Like coming home. Here is what it was composed of: faith, trust, knowing, patience, health, love (of life, self, immediates, God in all guises), creative fulfilment, material comfort and hope. And optimism. I once thought I had hope and optimism, but I saw now that in reality what I had was a yearning for any life but my own, to be anywhere but here and now. And a fervent belief that if I just kept willing it to do so, life would change.

I was soon to leave Italy and on the following Monday I had the thought, as I cycled to Mario's bar, that I was going to miss men in pastel pants. A bloke was cycling the opposite way to me down a lane and he looked fantastic. He was wearing a well-cut pair of lemon trousers, low slung at the hips and narrow at the ankle, teamed with a blue and lemon pinstriped shirt. *Ciao, bello.* Only in Italy.

'This Lord Byron,' said Mario. 'He also stayed a while in Montenero, *no*?'

It was true. He had taken a house in the hills above Livorno for a few months to beat the Pisan summer heat. I hadn't gone there, but I wasn't going to Genoa either. I felt my time roaming around Italy was up.

'I will take you to Montenero,' said Mario. 'We go tomorrow.'

It was only a half hour's drive, but a world away from Pisa. 'Truly, he had an eye for real estate,' I said to Mario. We had driven to the tiny town of Montenero, taken the steep little funicular up to a Catholic sanctuary where a portrait of the Madonna performed many miracles, and we now sat perched at an airy lookout affording views over the seaside sprawl of Livorno, then across the Ligurian Sea towards Corsica. There was bougainvillea in bloom and cypress trees whispered a deep, long exhale.

'Yes, it is very beautiful,' said Mario. 'What is the most beautiful place in Italy you have been?'

'Rome,' I said. 'No question. Saint Peter's is the most sublime thing I have ever seen.'

'Ah, Vaticano,' he said reverentially. 'I hope to go one day.'

'You haven't been to Rome?' I was stunned. And then I felt bad. He looked embarrassed and said nothing. 'Well, you have all the time in the world to go. And you must.'

Something shifted then. I saw the vast difference in our life experiences.

'Why you follow this man? You never tell me why,' intuitive but inexperienced Mario asked.

'Because he is, for me, a person who lived truth. I want to live truth. And you know what? I've learned to do it, following him. I really have.'

'You not live truth before?'

I let out a big sigh, in time with the cypress trees.

'Tell me, Julietta, why you not married?'

'So many reasons. Not through deliberate choice. But still, I chose it.' I was not sure he understood.

We were both silent for a while.

'You deserve happy.'

Maybe he did understand, after all.

'Now *that*, I do know. Yes, Mario, I know that now.'

He took my hand and we sat and watched that azure view sparkle and change as the clouds moved and the breeze blew, and misty air currents drifted across it.

'I will miss you very much when you go,' he said.

My crush deepened then, to an immense respect. He saw, as clearly as I did in that moment, what was right for me. And what wasn't. And I knew what I wanted: someone to walk next to me along life's path, not behind or in front. Otherwise, I would walk it alone. And assuredly, confidently, contentedly so.

I left Pisa, on the train for Florence, with one emotion: gratitude. And maybe that was all I needed.

My Florence hotel, the Regency, was a genteel affair on a big green *piazza* with a carousel in the middle of it and surrounded by wide, well-maintained footpaths and villas of grace and elegance, not a piece of peeling paint in sight, not a skerrick of crumbling plaster. It looked more like London's Bloomsbury than Italy.

I walked straight from my hotel to the Duomo, coming at it from the rear, where there was hardly anyone. I stood next to that ornate wonder of a cathedral in a big, sunshine-drenched corner of *piazza* that I had all to myself, opened my arms out wide, turned my face up to the sun, and let a sense of achievement reign. A nice moment for me, if a touch alarming for the—thankfully few—passers-by.

Florence delivered fantastic gelato straight off the bat. Ridiculous. New favourite flavour, *mandarino* from Coronas Gelateria, not far from the Piazza della Signoria. It was true, after all. How I felt about this place really was about my state of mind. I loved Florence now.

Later, I was sitting at dinner when a letter to Lord Byron appeared in my notebook.

Dear Lord Byron,

I had no idea, in truth, why I set out after you in the beginning. I wasn't even looking for an idea when you landed on my head. But once I let the idea of you in, the quickening was astounding. Miracles began dropping in. It moved forward so fast. I had no time to reconsider. I am still unsure as to who picked whom and why. It seems trite to thank you after all I've been through and I have no words to come close to the gratitude I feel. So I might just use the words you once wrote to your good friend and travelling companion, Cam Hobhouse.

You are my friend, 'one whom I have known long, and accompanied far, whom I have found wakeful over my sickness and kind in my sorrow, glad in my prosperity and firm in my adversity, true in counsel and trusty in peril—to a friend often tried and never found wanting ...'

Thank you, Lord Byron.

On my way back to my hotel, I decided to walk a different route to the way I'd come.

I was slurping on unbelievably excellent gelato, new flavour of fig, which I got from a place called Festival del Gelato as an after-dinner punctuation mark. When I needed to discard my cup I opened one of the street-side bins, such as had been the bane of my Pisan existence. To my amazement, it was a silent bin. It had constructs on the side of the lid that eased it up and down, thus avoiding noisy slamming. I was so taken with it I tried every bin I passed. Way to go, Florence. Now, to invent the silent bottle.

Strolling up a peaceful residential road, I came across a space lit by candles and furnished in a not-too-shabby shabby-chic style. It was a tiny exquisite hotel. I walked in. The design spoke to me. The vibe made me feel like it was home. It was how I wanted my life to look. A friendly man behind the desk showed me through the beautifully decorated public rooms, to much oohing and aahing from me. I told him that next time I was in Florence I would stay there.

As we came back into the lobby he handed me a brochure. It revealed the name of the place to be The J and J Hotel. I am known to many, if not most people, as JJ.

Walking out, I heard music ahead. A gospel choir was in a *piazza* singing, an unusual thing to find in Italy. They were doing a fine, swinging job of 'This Little Light of Mine', a song I regularly sang to myself to help let my little light shine.

I got to the square where they were doing their impromptu

performance and where a crowd of people were gathered, hanging out, listening, enjoying the night, and I sang and clapped along, and promised myself that as much as I could, I would always let my little light shine.

Waking in the middle of the night, I realised there was poetry in that walk home. Maybe it was Lord Byron's letter back to me. The silent bins certainly suggested his sense of humour ...

I took the train to Rome and as soon as I arrived I knew once and for all that the city dotted the 'i' and crossed the 't' in 'love it' for me. It energised me immediately. I was only staying in a decent room near the railway station in transit, but even there, I felt a different kind of alive. The exhilaration was so significant because I had yet to find it anywhere else. Rome was home for me. *A* home, anyway, and here's what I knew about home. I would never give up looking for home, spiritual and physical. I believed it was in the journeying, openly, optimistically, hopefully, courageously, that I was finding out who I truly was. And that, of course, was really home.

I hadn't intended to go out in Rome, as I'd arrived late and had an early train to catch. But I couldn't resist visiting my fat little friend, the Pantheon. On the way, I came to Piazza Sant'Ignazio, an apricot and pale-blue perfection of jigsaw-puzzle-piece Baroque buildings around a Corinthian columnal church dedicated to the founder of the Jesuits. There was a restaurant there with outdoor tables and, before I knew it, I'd asked to be seated. A *signora* put me at a table with a great view of the church. A huge edifice, with elegant scrolls and candles made of stone at the top, its little angels in mischievous motion, holding up a shield above the door, captured my attention. I watched the setting sun change them from cream to yellow, through deepening shades of orange. The antipasti were delicious: buffalo mozzarella, olives, artichokes, the bread dense with a snappy crust, the house vino a nice drop from Montepulciano. Handsome men gave me the look, as only Italian men can. Women of my age looked in another way that said, *I couldn't do what you are doing, sitting there by yourself, but I wish I could.* It was one of the best meals of my life.

'You deserve happy,' Mario had said to me. That quick jolt of Roma energy made me think that city might be where I would find that happy. It was a possibility for me—and who knew? Maybe I'd move there and invite Mario for a visit. It was time to make plans for the future, my future of choice.

Very early the next morning I boarded the train to Brindisi in Puglia, where I would board an overnight public ferry to the Ionian island of Cephalonia.

It wasn't the slow travel of Lord Byron, but it was slowish travel. It was a six-hour train trip. *Dio mio*, the scenery. We passed through the arid otherworldliness of Puglia and all I could think was that I adored this country. With my soul.

Later, from the deck of a Greek ferry, I watched Italy's coast glittering as the sun set behind it while we sailed north along it. I felt no sadness to be leaving. The ache of love and longing. But no sadness. I knew I would be back. But moreover, I knew, with every atom in my body, that Italy was part of me and I it. It had been the backdrop of remarkable transformation for me. And even if I never went back, it would always, always, remain a base ingredient in the essence of me. It was true love that I felt for Italy. I think it loved me back.

20

Greece

Well—well, the world must turn upon its axis,
And all mankind turn with it, heads or tails,
And live and die, make love and pay our taxes,
And as the veering wind shifts, shift our sails;
The king commands us, and the doctor quacks us,
The priest instructs, and so our life exhales,
A little breath, love, wine, ambition, fame,
Fighting, devotion, dust,—perhaps a name.

Don Juan, Canto II

Sailing along the Italian coast, the *Hercules* had to draw into land three times for bad weather and repairs. In Livorno, then called Leghorn, Lord Byron met with Greeks and was dismayed to learn their main concern was money, not glory. Though the journey had its light moments and though Lord Byron clearly enjoyed strutting the deck in the brass-buttoned uniform he'd had made for the journey, sudden episodes of darkness would come over him, a foreboding perhaps.

Two weeks after leaving Genoa, Lord Byron arrived at the port of Argostoli on the island of Cephalonia. The Ionians were then under British rule. Preparing for war, preparing for Greece, he had inadvertently found himself in a situation that was comforting and familiar. He would be six months there. His days were spent planning and strategising, but also partaking of English colonial life. On Cephalonia he became painfully aware of the complexities and seemingly insurmountable difficulties that would face him on the Greek mainland. But there was also a welcoming back into English society. He attended dinners and drinks and won the admiration of British military men and other officials, representatives of aspects of his home life he had come to criticise and rail against. Now, he found himself delighting in salons, picnics and in his own welcome by people who might have once believed the worst of him.

But the Greek cause remained at the forefront of his thoughts. While funding and finding housing for refugees, he met fifteen-year-old Loukas, who became his page, and a lamentable love. At the same time, he experienced rising panic about how foreign his surviving daughter, Ada, was now to him, which he expressed in letters to Augusta. Lord Byron always needed someone to love and love him back, especially when his insecurities arose. Though Byron fell for the young man, lavishing gifts and attention on him, his affections were not returned. However, while Lord Byron had all but given up poetry by now, Loukas did inspire a few final, lovely bursts.

Two days before the end of 1823 he set off, finally, for the Peloponnese and strategically crucial Messolonghi, a swampy city on the Gulf of Patras. On 5 January 1824 he disembarked wearing a scarlet military jacket and full regalia, hoping to put forward an appearance of authority and inspire faith. He was soon to find a not unexpected harshness to life there: the landscape itself, malarial and dank; the mood of the people, bleak; the threats on the horizon, ominous; the constant stream of military seeking his aid, relentless; the beseeching for money, duplicitous; the demanding of his support, genuine but complex.

On 22 January 1824 Lord Byron turned thirty-six. Three weeks later he fell deliriously ill. He recovered, but by the latter stages of March, with many plans for action in the war thwarted or abandoned, spring rains set in. Lord Byron's need for physical exertion saw him set out riding despite the inclemency. On the evening of 9 April, after riding through a deluge, he fell terribly ill again and collapsed. Two doctors, both members of his party, both inexperienced, recommended bleeding; Byron refused. As he was worse the next day, one of the doctors fed him castor oil, causing him diarrhoea. Again bleeding was recommended, again refused. The next day, he was well enough to ride again. The following day he was worse still. By 16 April, he acquiesced to being bled. His speech became incoherent, his fever off the scale. On 17 April they fed him purgatives and bled him again. On 18 April, Easter Sunday, winds howled and rain pelted. Lord Byron was in spasms, vomiting and moving in and out of delirium. He consented, though not with any conviction, to more bleeding. The doctors put leeches on his forehead. Some time during that day, he spoke his final coherent words. Becoming conscious of the gathered mournful around his bed he said, '*Oh, questa è una bella scena*', oh, this is a beautiful scene. He was unconscious for the next twenty-four hours, breathing with difficulty, convulsing. In the seconds before he died, on 19 April, he opened his eyes and closed them again. And that was it.

Though of course, not. The hoopla surrounding his untimely death reads not unlike that surrounding Princess Diana's: theories and blame-shifting over the cause, regrets from those who had turned on him, accusations from his cronies and, worst of all, the burning of his autobiography by a committee of his closest who felt the contents too hot, both for the sake of his reputation and probably their own. The refusal of the crown to have him buried at Westminster Abbey, crowds of people, weighted towards female, along the funereal route as his body was taken to the family plot for burial. A celebrity to the last, and beyond.

His legacy is complex, like his life. Dichotomies abound: love and hate, light and darkness, the sublime and the ridiculous. In that, it is a complete life. One lived at the edge of passion, pushing itself to its extreme, for better or worse, a blazing beacon of gusto. And self-acceptance of a sort. He took pride in his strengths, and remained aware of his weaknesses. And though he did not resolve or even try to remedy his failings, he saw them, and himself, as part of a greater whole, part of a world that is, after all, ambiguous itself.

To be ourselves, flaws and all, to be not fearless, but courageous in the face of all of whom we are, I think that's all that's asked of us. And I think Lord Byron shone, and still shines, as a courageous soul in full expression. *Oh, questa è una bella vita.*

I can think of no more beautiful a life than his.

It was 6 a.m. on a July morning. My approach—through a narrow gulf between the islands of Ithaca and Cephalonia— was mystical. There was no moon but the morning star was bright and big. It was pulsating, or seemed to, through the air currents. The islands were solemn black monoliths, save for little patches of twinkling lights. There was a rainbow glow around Ithaca, like the rainbow glow around Jesus' head in the mosaics at Ravenna's San Vitale, my favourite of that city's churches. God was in full, unsubtle expression that morning. It looked like the dawn of time. The ferry glided silently through placid water, like it was travelling through space.

I had watched Italy's coast until dark, eaten some dinner, gone to sleep in my little cabin and then, suddenly, I was in Greece.

Though I sailed to Sami on the east coast of Cephalonia, not Argostoli to the west as he did, I felt a sense of Lord Byron as soon as I got to the island. It was so very early and a café had opened up on the main street along the water, selling coffee and pastries to the sleepy coming ashore. I sat on the water's edge reading about Lord Byron from Fiona McCarthy's wonderful book, waiting for a man called Melis from a car hire place called Greekstones, apparently a Flintstones reference, to come and pick me up.

I realised that, early on, I'd misread Lord Byron's affinity with the Greek people, thinking he was only in the Greek cause for the glory. Now I had come to know Lord Byron. He was not in anything only for the glory. I could also understand his affinity with the Greek people. They were worry free in some ways, frenetic in others, a fun, down-to-earth bunch with a robust spirituality and a love of life. Hard not to love. I knew. My longest relationship, of seven years, had been with a man of Greek heritage. I didn't pretend to understand their character entirely, but I definitely knew a thing or two about their psyche from that relationship. It took coming to Cephalonia to remember that, and to realise it was an aspect of that relationship which I actually cherished: that window, often intense and complicated, into another culture.

I did not believe it a coincidence that windows into other cultures were what I had sought in my writing ever since that relationship ended. We are the sum of our experiences. To regret was to deny that. It didn't mean sugar-coating memories or denying damage or hurt. It was about seeing the divine plan and, in the places where that was not possible, understanding there were greater forces at work and trusting, when all was said and done, that they knew what they were doing.

The divine plan seemed obvious on Cephalonia from the get-go. Melis picked me up and drove me from the middle of the island's east side to his office near the south-western cul-de-sac in which I would be staying.

I had booked my accommodation because it was the only place meeting my requirements: cheap. Cephalonia was a big island, the biggest of the Ionians, with lots of villages and choice of accommodation. I booked somewhere, completely unwittingly, virtually in the next village along from Lord Byron's, Metaxas. As Cephalonia's settlements were in clusters with big stretches of undeveloped landscape in between, this was yet another phenomenal confluence.

Just as Lord Byron was assimilated back into English life on that island, the same thing was happening to me—sort of. The island of Cephalonia was still awash with English, for a start, and Tony and Sheila, who owned the B&B in which I would stay, were about as English as they come.

The B&B was hard to find, though. I found the village all right; Melis had been very clear with his directions. As we drove to his office, he pointed out navigational aids: an old ruined castle high on a hill, an old olive tree in the middle of an intersection, a Fiat dealership. When he handed over the keys to my little car, he reiterated his directions—to the village. Melis did not know where the house was either. I reached the village, then stopped and asked directions of a young woman and her father, who was in a hat my dad would have killed for. It was a beaten-up Akubra-style deal with a band of what looked like feral cat fur around the crown. 'There are some English people up there,' the girl motioned from the main road to the village proper. 'We wish we could help you further but we can't.'

After a while, I wished they could too.

I drove up a tiny hilly road, around a corner, into a cluster of houses and then down a tiny hilly road and back to where I started. I found a handsome silver-haired Greek man with a leaf blower and excellent English. 'Do you know the Villa Jocomai?' I asked. This was the name of the B&B. The silver fox looked thoughtful.

'You know? I think I do. You work enough around the place, you read all the signs, you get to know things.' I didn't think he realised exactly how sage that statement was. He directed me back up the first tiny road. Follow it to the church. Go left after the church. It's a yellow house. I tried this several times. On about the fifth attempt, the silver fox had made his way up to the churchyard, where he was now eating in the shade.

'Left after the church, simple,' he reiterated, after I stopped to ask directions again and allowed him his amusement at the fact that I was still cruising the neighbourhood half an hour after our first meeting.

I drove on a short distance until I heard 'Stoooooop!' The silver fox was running along the side of the church. I slammed on the brakes. He motioned up the goat track behind the church. 'Go left here!'

That was a road?

I found the Villa Jocomai. Past some crumbled stone ruins overrun with cactus, beyond a tiny old cemetery, then amid olive groves and fields stretching up to the imposing black sweep of Mount Anos was a suburban-looking home, painted, yes indeed, yellow.

Sheila answered the door. She was a tiny, cute, tanned blonde woman in shorts and a bikini top. She invited me in and led me out through the kitchen to the back garden. Her doppelgänger daughter in the same outfit was having a cup of tea and a ciggie on the back porch. Sheila's husband, Tony, was scooping dead wasps out of the small above-ground pool. Everyone was berry brown. The grandson of Sheila and Tony, a four-year-old with glasses and a spiky haircut, was dancing around me.

This was not the way I normally did things, let alone how I had spent the past several months. It was about as far removed from that as you could get. I was off-balance.

'How was your trip?' Sheila handed me a mug of tea. I must have gone into my old pattern, belittling my experiences to make myself smaller, and so, likeable, because the next thing she said was, 'So you didn't have a very good time, then?' as she lit up another cigarette.

I corrected myself. 'I have had the most incredible life-changing time and I am beyond grateful for it.'

Sheila led me to my room, a small space at the end of a hallway. We were all sharing the bathrooms. The house was not air-conditioned. The sun hit the shutters all afternoon. It was forty-two degrees centigrade.

I left the family scene in search of water, and swam in clear aqua sea, the likes of which I'd only ever seen on postcards and even then, I thought it was Photoshopped. I adore the ocean generally but, *mamma mia*, this was some ocean to love. I ducked and dived and frolicked like a dolphin.

When I came back, Tony and Sheila's daughter and grandson had left on their journey back to their home in England. Tony and Sheila were on the front terrace having an evening tipple and fags, Sheila rosé and lemonade, Tony a beer. I joined them for a rosé before heading off to dinner, where I watched the sun go down across a perfect ocean view and listened to Greek music played live splendidly well. One of the musicians sent me over a drink. It was ouzo and Solo and it tasted like dishwashing liquid. It was an appreciated gesture, though. I did think Stella had finally got her groove back.

Back at the Villa Jocomai, Tony and Sheila were still on the terrace. The house was ringing with sixties pop music played loud. 'We like to listen to the oldies,' said Tony. Clearly. It was a case of not beating them, but joining them, because even with my new ability to sleep through noise, hard-won from my rounds with Pisa's garbos, Sheila and Tony's oldies would have woken a hibernating bear. But they were convivial and lively conversationalists and we stayed up way too late talking about island life, life in our home countries, places we'd travelled, religion, politics and cricket. Pretty much the same ground Lord Byron covered while on Cephalonia too.

Like Lord Byron as he left Italy, I couldn't help but feel that something had ended. I had found and confronted what I needed to in my heart. However, while Lord Byron was preparing for war on Cephalonia, I'd won my war. I no longer had a desire or need to prove anything.

And so now maybe I could have that holiday. I drove the island's length, stopping to swim in that ocean when I felt the need. I sat at the little memorial square next to the place where Lord Byron's house was before it was totalled by an earthquake in the 1950s, and I soaked in the sheer beauty of the view he would have had across the deep blue Ionian Sea, the soft breeze, the profound gratitude I felt for having the opportunity to be there. I was settling into myself. It was a wonderful feeling.

My last night on Cephalonia, Tony and Sheila took me out to their favourite Greek taverna. I got a little excited and drank way too much Greek white wine. But we were high on a hill overlooking that dazzling ocean and rugged island, it had been an insanely hot day and the evening cool was making me come alive. Plus, Tony and Sheila were a hoot. This was life. This was how I wanted it to be. We laughed and sang and clapped along to the Greek music and when Sheila got up to do traditional Greek dancing, I remembered. Joie de vivre, that's what I remembered.

The restaurant was crawling with kids. 'You'd be a good mum,' Tony said as he watched me chat to a bunch of them.

'Maybe a step-mum one day,' I said, warmly, optimistically. Not the slightest bit wistful. I had that feeling again of having stepped into life. Of getting on with it.

At 7 a.m. on the morning of my leaving Cephalonia, Melis from Greekstones was waiting for me at his office to take me to the ferry after I returned my car. Driving down the rugged, dry mountain into Sami, Melis said, 'Look at all the butterflies.' They were everywhere, alongside us and above us on that windy, rocky road, flying out of and fluttering about the limestone road's edge that was jagged in cubes like potato salad, garnished by cypress and olive trees.

Ever since my mum died, seeing butterflies in unexpected places has been a sign for me, of love and reassurance, of her presence. I wondered when Melis said that. Then he added, in quite an awestruck tone, softly, thoughtful, almost to himself, 'It's very unusual. Rhodes has a lot of butterflies, but not usually here.'

And then I knew.

I boarded the ferry for the mainland of Greece with butterflies dancing in my heart. After a spectacular three-hour cruise through the Ionians, I got to the delightfully untouristy town of Patras and checked into my hotel where I slept a sound, peaceful sleep.

The next day, I took the bus to Messolonghi. I needed to get a sense of where Lord Byron died. His house had been on the ocean's edge. I knew it was no longer there so I just headed for the water and sat on the end of a pier.

I settled in with *Don Juan* and began to read some of his sublime stanzas. I looked up, gazed across the pancake flat water and reflected: in circles I had known, poetry had that stigma of being a naïve undergrad pastime; the pretentious posturing of young blossoming minds with intellectual aspirations—kids who took themselves way too seriously. How I had sold my experiences—and myself—short, labelling the things I loved as a kid 'phases' or fancies to be affectionately scoffed at from the grand viewpoint of maturity. I used to draw too and found sweet silence in it. Sitting out the back of my mum's house, in the garden, focusing on a thing, or copying pictures from the old copies of *Life* magazine that were stored under the house.

In the turning away from my passions for language, art, spirituality, I had begun to lose myself. And now I had found myself again.

And then I had the urge ... for the first time in thirty years. I tried to shove it down, but no, there was no shoving down now. It was the least I could do to honour Lord Byron, here in Messolonghi, where the champion of my heart had died.

I put down *Don Juan*, picked up my notebook, and wrote a poem.

I didn't know if it was any good, but it felt good to write it and that was good enough for me. I was different. I could say for the first time in my forties that I felt my age and that was not a bad thing, but a truly accomplished, positive feeling. It filled me, head to toe. I felt proud of who I was, how far I had come, where I was. I was in no danger from me. I was in good hands.

I was in no danger from me. I was in good hands. This was a concept so new it made me gasp out loud when I thought it.

I had spent my adult life not trusting myself to do the right thing. I had spent all this time trying to trust God when I had no trust of myself. I had never seen this before.

I trusted me to fulfil my needs. I trusted myself to create the life I desired. I trusted myself to take care of me. To keep me safe. To see me thrive.

I knew myself. Yes, it felt good.

I got up to go and catch the bus back to Patras, but before I left the pier, I turned and blew a final, grateful kiss into the water to Lord Byron. And to my mum, and my dad. But also, to me.

Epilogue

And so. Three months after my return to Australia, here I am in Byron Bay, this new version of me, about to go on this date. I walk out the gates of the apartment complex and two large black butterflies dance across my path, so close their wings almost touch my nose. These butterflies let me know I am supported. I cross the road to the beach, kick off my shoes and walk slowly along the sand from Belongil to Byron township. The sun is softer as the evening settles in and people are out walking dogs, body surfing, splashing in the shallows. It is idyllic. Everything sparkles. I feel like even I am. Then it hits me for the first time: I am meeting this man in the most aptly named place possible, Byron Bay. And I am meeting this man whose name is Gabriel, the name my mother was also christened, in the feminine form, Gabrielle. And now I think about it, in the photo I have seen of this Gabriel, he has long dark curly hair, thick lips and a cleft chin, not at all unlike Lord Byron himself.

Now I am getting a bit silly with the signs. But the thing is, I hadn't gone on that dating site looking for someone. That was not my expectation. Getting on there was more an act of affirmation: an 'if you build it, they will come' exercise. You've got to be in it to win it. And there he was. And there I was.

Whatever *this* was, it felt full of possibility, full of goodness.

I thought back to my conversation with Angie earlier at the apartment. 'Of course you're feeling nervous,' she'd said. 'But you have to get yourself out there. You have to take a chance with your heart. You're nervous because this could be something good. And even if it's not, what's really good is that you're ready for this. You're nervous because whatever this is, it's a new beginning. This is the moment. It's the difference between giving up and saying you deserve it. Saying you deserve to have someone in your life who gives a shit about what kind of day you had.'

She had me teary again then.

'Now, go put some perfume on.'

And suddenly, I am in a blue dress and Acqua di Parma, waiting for a man called Gabriel in the beer garden of the Beach Hotel. He comes from the direction of the Norfolk pines with the cooling evening eastern sky behind him. He is looking for me. I walk towards him. He sees me and he grins. And I keep moving towards him. I keep moving forward because it is all I can do now.

Coda

For the curious, for Lord Byron, who would no doubt consider me a coward if I didn't publish this, and for the sake of completion— here is that poem I wrote in Messolonghi.

I AM NOT FLAWLESS, BUT PERFECT AS IS
Stanzas on Self

I

I am not flawless, but perfect as is.
I am God's ideal, this truth life's basis.
What once I believed to be heresy
I understand as the divine mercy.

II

My mistakes shall lead me to what is right.
The only way through may be a dark night
Of the soul. Oh, blessed blackness. I bow
Humbled. How great the knowledge you bestow.

III

Loneliness shows me how much I am loved.
In a breath's drawing all that I covet
Is revealed, a pause perchance to listen.
Angel's wings beat. Truth is all that is, then.

IV

All are growing pains, rips in the tissue
Of the spirit. Let then God's work ensue.
Imbuing self wholly in the feeling,
I receive greater strength from the healing.

V

I have love to give. Let the world have it
Now. No longer a slave to decrepit
Notions of needing the one to endow
It to, I set it free, my flow, its flow.

VI

I am puzzle in progress, not finished
Even when, brightness dimmed, this skin is shed.
Pieces yet to be formed count infinite—
To mind mystery, to soul intimate.

VII

There can never be too much me. Who said
I laughed too loud? How I elicited
This notion, well, there's no need for the how.
From less than myself, here, all of me, now.

VIII

At the end I can say I gave my life
My heart. Not always. It's true I have been rife
With doubts that debilitated gravely.
Proud then, by grace, that I've risen bravely.

IX

I am far from fearless, but not afraid
To face my fear. In the endless parade
Of dreaded demons, all my creation,
Marches truth, marches God and salvation.

X

God is all I need, all I ever am,
Ever was, will be, ad infinitum.
May I keep God close and so close keep me,
His image, my life its epitome.

Acknowledgments

Thanks to Colette Vella, Kay Scarlett and Elizabeth Cowell at Pier 9 and Murdoch Books; Selwa Anthony, agent; Anouska Jones, editor.

Diana Stainlay and Terry Mooney at Singapore Airlines, Florence Pasquier and Alexis Darne at Rail Europe, Luke Starr and ICG Hotels for kindnesses without which I could not have followed Byron so.

In Greece, Tony and Sheila Curtis.

In Italy, Alessandro and Dario Dal Corso, Cinzia Fanciulli, *bellissima* Nina Fiorenza, Rosanna Genovese, Paola, Luciana and everyone at A Casa di Paola. And of course, the makers of *gelati artigianale*. Long may you scoop.

Special thanks to my family for the unique perspective and for loving support, Quentin, Marg and Liam, Dale, Damien, Regina, Sinead, Paul, Sean, Vera, Claryssa, Orien, and lovely Erin, whose story is my story in many aspects, and Bernadette and Andrew who go to the barricades for me time and again and without whom I wonder whether I would have survived.

A big thanks to Michelle Singer, Angie Kelly and Sarah Maguire for encouragement, friendship and purchase orders.

I'd like to acknowledge all the biographers of Byron whose work fuelled this journey. It was a joy to read you. A particular suggestion for further reading is Fiona McCarthy's brilliant

Byron: Life and Legend, John Murray (Publishers) Ltd, 2002.

And thank you George Noel Gordon, Lord Byron, for sharing your light, even when it seemed the whole world was trying to smother it.